RAISING CHILDREN YOU CAN LIVE WITH

A GUIDE FOR FRUSTRATED PARENTS

JAMIE RASER

Bayou Publishing

HOUSTON, TEXAS

Copyright © 1999
by Jamie Raser

This publication is designed to provide accurate and authoritative infor-mation with regard to the subject matter covered. It is sold with the un-derstanding that the publisher is not engaged in rendering legal, accounting, psychotherapeutic, or other professional service. If expert as-sistance is required, the services of a competent professional person should be sought. *From a Declaration of Principles jointly adopted by a Committee of the American Bar Association and a Committee of Publish-ers.*

Printed in the United States of America

Library of Congress Catalog Card Number: 98-88660

**Publisher's Cataloging-in-Publication
(Provided by Quality Books, Inc.)**
Raser, Jamie.
        Raising children you can live with : a guide for frustrated parents / by Jamie Raser.—2nd ed.
        p.   cm.
    Includes bibliographical references.
    ISBN: 1-886298-11-4
    1. Child rearing. I. Title.
HQ769.R37   1999   649.1
                                                QBI98-1383

Cover design by Eric Norton at Jenkins Group
Drawings by Cynthia Burtch. Printed by permission

Published by: Bayou Publishing
                        2524 Nottingham
                        Houston, TX 77005-1412
                        (713) 526-4558
                        http://www.bayoupublishing.com

Praise for this Book...

"An excellent resource for clinicians and families."

—Randy Phelps, Ph.D.
Past-President of Houston Psychological Association

"Sound ideas for improving parent-child relationships. Strategic interaction and the Parent's Creed are invaluable tools for parents, foster parents, and all those in the parenting role."

—Janet Legler Luft,
Program Specialist, Children's Protective Services,
Department of Protective and Regulatory Services

"I found this book to be very 'real' in its focus. (In fact, I feel like you must have been hiding in a closet in my house.) I will be able to use many of the suggested techniques in both my professional and personal interactions."

—Judy Connors,
Assistant Principal, Junior High School

"Patients are always asking me for advice with their children. This book, with its clear, easy-to-read examples, hits the spot. I freely recommend this book to my patients."

—Paul Millea, M.D.,
Family Physician

Contents

Acknowledgments

Since the publication of the first version of *Raising Children You Can Live With*, many people have supported and helped my efforts to improve the lives of both parents and teenagers.

The ideas have been sharpened in some areas and expanded in others in large part because of the feedback I've gotten from hundreds of parents, teachers, and therapists.

My publisher, Victor Loos, has always been supportive and encouraging. This has been an exciting and educational joint venture.

Sue, my wife, has been forever behind me—helping, inspiring and taking care of our child when I needed to work on the book.

Rhonda George and Judy King have provided supportive and invaluable editing suggestions which I've certainly needed.

All of my colleagues at the Houston Galveston Institute, from interns to faculty, have kept my mind active and hungry for new ideas.

Numerous teachers, counselors, administrators, and families in the Deer Park (Texas) Independent School District have provided opportunities to hone my interactional skills, clarify my ideas, and experiment with interventions. I am forever in their debt.

Cameron's wonderful smile makes my day complete.

This book is not about "how to raise children" as if there is only one way—mine. There are as many ways to raise children as there are parents, families, and cultures.

However, when the relationship with your child is not going as well as you would like, when you are miserable as a parent and your children seem miserable too, this book may help you understand how things went wrong and how you can make them better.

*Parenting is not something you **do to** a child; it is a relationship you have **with** a child.*

—Jamie Raser,
Parenting with Success Workshop,
Humble I.S.D. (1993)

Foreword

The solution is not to "get tougher," but to get more effective!

Children can draw parents into interactions that become Us (the children) against Them (authority figures), not Us against the realistic and logical consequences of rules. Us against Them becomes a war. "Getting tougher" can win battles, but it may also teach that winning is the most important goal and that force and power are the ways to win. Children then learn that, with enough power, they can also win and that this is how the world operates. If they feel they are losing, they simply apply more power; they do not learn to accept losing.

Rules then become unimportant. Power is everything. Children will learn how to gain and respect power, not how to respect rules or authority. Thus, gangs, guns, and violence proliferate.

This book teaches parents how to be in control of situations and interactions rather than how to be in control of children. When parents are in control of themselves and the interactions, children will learn to control themselves!

Raising Children You Can Live With is based on the premise that when parents stay out of interactional battles with children, the children are more likely to learn the life lessons they need. Getting into interactional wars will ultimately teach the wrong kinds of lessons. This book explains these concepts and explains how to stay out of the battles. It gives detailed examples of 13 of the serious situations that can develop between parents and children and how to handle them so that a positive outcome is possible while a more positive and enjoyable relationship is established.

We need people in our society who can act with intelligence, ethics, morality, and concern. Most of our children already have these qualities. It is up to the parents and adult society to interact with our children in such a way that these qualities can come out.

—Jamie Raser

Children today are tyrants.

—Socrates (390 BC)

Section 1

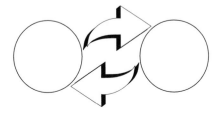

All anybody expects of an adolescent is that he act like an adult and be satisfied to be treated like a child.

—Anonymous

Chapter 1

The Parenting Relationship

Parenting is not a series of "techniques" or "manipulations" designed to gain control over another human being. It is a special kind of relationship between a parent and a child.[1]

That relationship is what ties you and your child together. It is the conduit for everything you give to and receive from your child. It is made up of the thousands of interactions you have together. As the interactions go, so goes the relationship.

You may gain momentary power or control by using various "tricks" as a parent, but **ongoing, permanent influence is achieved through effective interactions. It is a product of relating successfully.** This book presents information about how parents and chil-

---

[1.] To avoid the awkward s/he and her/him, the implied sex of the child and the parent in the text will be alternated.

dren relate to each other, how that relationship can go wrong, how negative interactions can lead to destructive behavior in children, and how to counteract a negative cycle.

Components of the Parent-Child Relationship

What are some of the components of your relationship with your child? Here are just a few of them:

> *Discipline*
>
> *Limits*
>
> *Caring*
>
> *Guidance*
>
> *Structure*
>
> *Love*
>
> *Instruction*
>
> *Respect*
>
> *Socialization*

In your relationship with your child you play different roles. These can generally be separated into roles considered to be "Business" and those considered to be "Personal" (see Figure 1).

As a parent and caretaker of a young, developing person, there are certain things you must teach your child so that he may function well in society and so that your home and family may run smoothly. You must set certain standards and limits for his behavior. These functions fall into what could be called the Business side of the relationship.

The other part of the relationship is the Personal side. This is where the fun, loving, caring, respectful part of the relationship is played out.

> ### The Parenting Relationship
>
> | BUSINESS | PERSONAL |
> |----------|----------|
> | Discipline | Caring |
> | Guidance | Love |
> | Structure | Respect |
> | Instruction | Fun |
> | Rules | Socializing |
> | Socialization | Friendship |

Figure 1: *Components of every parenting relationship*

Sometimes parents pay so much attention to the Business side of the relationship that they forget the Personal side. Or they may feel they can't allow the fun, friendly part because it will somehow weaken the Business (i.e., rules) side of the relationship. Children who seem to need lots of structure often provide little that is rewarding in the relationship. The relationship is dominated by the Business side to the exclusion of the Personal side. For instance, you may have found yourself saying, "He never gives me a chance to do anything but be the mean ogre that he thinks I am."

You can discipline *and* use the Personal side too. In fact, if you feel all you can do is the Business side, you might be surprised at the benefits of bringing in the Personal side or at least making a sincere effort to do so. It may take some creativity on your part, but think about it. If you're not enjoying the relationship because all you're doing is yelling, setting limits, and enforcing rules, then your child is probably not enjoying the relationship either. If your child is always mad at you and sees you only as the Ruler, he is much less likely to want to cooperate. He will not be inclined to obey any rules you have. If your child gets some of the friendship, love, or respect that can come from the Personal side, he may also be more willing to make concessions. He may be more ready to do what is necessary to continue to live in this pleasant atmosphere.

However, just as you can concentrate too much on the Business side, you can also concentrate too much on the Personal side. You do have a job to do with your child. You are not merely a child's friend. She is not there to share your burdens. If you move too much in the direction of being a "buddy," you will have problems later on when you do need to set limits. Indeed, setting limits is a part of the task of socialization, which is part of the job of parenting.

Figure 2. *Effective parenting requires both the Business and the Personal sides. Problems emerge when one side outweighs the other.*

"Blurring" of the two separate sides of the parenting relationship occurs when, for example, a parent interprets a child's failure to obey a rule (a Business issue) as lack of respect for the parent (a Personal issue). Another example is when a parent feels he cannot have fun or cannot socialize in the relationship (a Personal issue) because he has to discipline his child (a Business issue).

In the corporate world, a business relationship is assumed. In a business relationship, if part of a contract is not performed, certain consequences are carried out. Usually there is not a feeling that the contract was broken because of personal reasons. If I contract with someone to paint my house on Monday and she doesn't show up, I probably will not think her failure to show up was because she did not like me. Nor would I pay her for her failure to do the work. Furthermore, I might be mad about it, but I would not give her a lecture about respecting my boundaries and rules. In other words, I would treat a business relationship like business and not introduce personal feelings into it.

Likewise, in parenting it is important to treat the Business side like business and simultaneously to use and enjoy the Personal side.

So how do you interact with your child in order to teach him all he needs to know while still being able to enjoy him? How do you relate from the Business side and still be the kind of person he enjoys?

Parents get locked into counterproductive interactions with their children that lead to destructive ways of thinking and acting, but a different way of thinking about interactions with children can help make those interactions more fun, fulfilling, and effective for both parent and child. By learning the mechanics of Strategic Interaction, you can become more effective in all of your interactions, whether they be with your child, your spouse, your own parents, your supervisor, your friend, or even yourself. And you will be able to change—even prevent—the destructive thought patterns and behaviors your child may get into.

Points to Remember
from Chapter 1

1. Permanent, ongoing influence is achieved through
  successful interactions and satisfying relationships,
  not through "power tactics."

2. There is a Business side and a Personal side to every
  parent-child relationship.

3. It is important to keep the Business and Personal
  sides separate.

4. Concentrating too much on either side of the relationship makes the relationship less effective and less fulfilling.

5. Children's destructive ways of thinking and acting
  stem from *interactions with* parents and other authority figures.

6. Effective use of *both* Business and Personal sides
  will lead to mutually satisfying relationships.

Trying to win a power struggle is like trying to win a nuclear war. You may achieve your goal, but not without heavy casualties on both sides.

—Jamie Raser,
Parents, Adolescents and Power Seminar (1993)

Chapter 2

Strategic Interaction

Interaction refers to the second-by-second, minute-by-minute, day-by-day contact you have with your child. All of those momentary contacts, when added together, form the relationship you have together. **Strategic Interaction** means that the interaction with your child can be *planned for a particular purpose*. The purpose should be to make the interactions, and thus the relationship, better. The goal is to interact in such a way that you will have more *influence* while also having more fun with and feeling closer to your child.

Look at Figure 3 on the next page. This symbolizes an interaction. The parent sends a message to her child, who then responds appropriately. The interaction goes smoothly and calmly. Right? For example, the parent says to her child, "Please clean up your room." Her child responds, "OK. Anything you say, parent dear." Right?

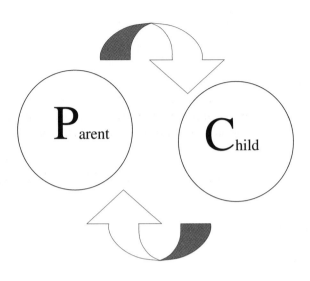

Figure 3. *Typical parent-child interaction.*

No? You mean it doesn't always go that way? Maybe it goes something like this:

   Parent: Please go clean up your room.

   Child: Quit telling me what to do.

   P: Don't take that tone of voice with me.

   C: It's my room. I'll keep it any way I want to.

   P: As long as you're living in this house, you'll follow my rules.
   It is not your room; it is my room and I say, "Clean it up
   now."

   C: I'll clean it when I'm good and ready. You can't boss me
   around.

   P: I won't discuss this anymore. You will clean it up now!

   C: Why don't you try and make me?

And on and on, ad nauseam. This kind of interaction is represented in Figures 4 through 6. It is a *negative reciprocal interaction.* It feeds on itself and gains speed and momentum going downhill fast. Do you ever have such an interaction with your child?

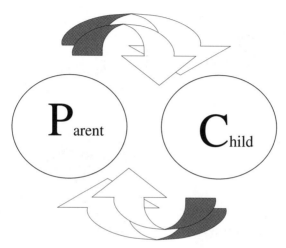

Figure 4. *Negative interactions generate more negative interactions.*

So what happened?

There are five parts of an interaction that you need to know in order to be able to understand, control, and use each interaction to your best parenting advantage. The five parts are **meaning, power, expression, deficit,** and **irrationality.**

Meaning

You may send what you think is a harmless request that can be acted upon easily. You may get back, though, immediate defensiveness and anger that seem inappropriate for the message you just sent. But where is the meaning in any message you send? Is it in the words you use or in the intention you have in mind when you send it? Neither. **The meaning of a message is in the interpretation of that message by the receiver.** You may help the receiver interpret it correctly through your choice of words, tone of voice, posture, attitude,

Figure 5. *Negative interactions continue to escalate and incorporate a growing reliance on power.*

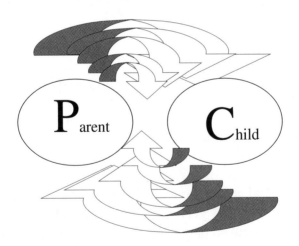

Figure 6. *As negative interactions build, they quickly become unmanageable.*

timing, and context. **However, the ultimate meaning is in the interpretation given by the other person.**

You can tell whether your message is interpreted the way you originally intended by the response sent back to you by the other person. In the example above, the defensive, angry response you received was a clue that your message was not interpreted as a simple, harmless request but as some sort of threat or authoritative command.

Figure 7. *What's going on when your "harmless" request is met with defensiveness and anger?*

Power

"Power," as used in this book, is a rather clear-cut concept. It has to do with whose wish will be dominant in an interaction. It involves the demand that the other person:

- do what you say,

- not do something else,

- change in some way, or

- become what you want him to be.

In the above example, the first demand is "Do what I say." It then becomes "Don't do what you are doing." Later in the cycle, it becomes "Change. Be a different kind of person" and "Be like I want you to be." All interactions that go badly, like the one above, involve at least some of these "power" elements.

Since power is an integral part of such interactions, who has the power in these negative interactions?

You, the parent, are older, wiser, better educated, and more worldly. You own the house the child lives in and the car he drives. You may have read numerous books on parenting. You have examined your own childhood and the parenting methods of your parents and of your friends. Your child is younger, smaller, weaker, and not nearly as knowledgeable about people. So who has the power?

In a negative interaction, it is not you! You want something from your child: cooperation, respect, or some sort of change.

Whenever you want something from someone else, you are in the weaker position because all the other person has to do is not do it!

Kids are great at finding ways not to do things. They can turn you down outright: "No!" Usually, though, they are more subtle. They say, "In a minute," "Later," or "OK," but then never do whatever you asked. They also may do what was requested, but they may do it very poorly or half-heartedly so that you feel it wasn't really done. Then you can argue about that.

Parent: You didn't do it.

Child: Yes, I did.

When you are in the whirlwind of a negative reciprocal interaction, both of you are struggling for power. You want something; your child refuses to do it. You want it even more; your child refuses again. You try harder and harder to get something; your child simply refuses.

So when you want something from your child, you are in the weaker position. This does not mean that you should never request anything from your child, but just remember that you are putting yourself in a more vulnerable position when you do. **You can learn to make requests in ways that are less likely to reduce your power and more likely to keep you from having to expend all your energy.**

When evaluating power struggles, pay attention to the *energy flow*. Who expends energy in interactions like the one we just looked at? You are developing logical arguments, yelling, thinking of punishments, getting frustrated, and feeling angry. What is your child doing? Maybe he is ignoring you while he calmly watches TV. Maybe he is simply saying "Whatever" with that "attitude." You want something from your child in such a way that he can simply refuse you. Who is expending energy? You are, most likely. That is another clue that you are in a power struggle and that you are losing. You are doing all the work; the child is doing nothing!

When the child has to pursue you, when the child has to worry about consequences and how to avoid them rather than your worrying about how to get something done, you have changed the energy flow. You are being more effective. However, this has to be done without increasing the power game or it will not last. I will give you practical suggestions on how to accomplish this in subsequent chapters. But first let's look at additional components of every interaction.

Expression

Another component of an interaction is **expression**. Something is being expressed by each of you in this interaction. You are expressing your wish for something to happen, your desire for the family to run smoothly, your wish for yourself to be respected, your hurt when that doesn't happen, your concern that she may not turn out well, and probably many other things. The simple request to clean the room suddenly becomes a very complicated, important interaction.

And what is the child expressing? Her simple "No!" may also mean, "I don't like being treated like a child" (a normal concern about changing roles), "I want freedom to make my own decisions" (freedom is a major issue for teens), "I don't want people controlling my life," "I want to experiment with being an adult," or "I'm trying to find my identity as a person separate from my parents and my family."

Again, the implicit things you are expressing to each other make all interactions both complicated and important. It becomes important for both of you to win the power struggle because to do so means that you are being "heard" by the other one. It means that your deep desires and fears are being acknowledged and understood.

Deficits

Power and expression are so important that if they are not handled to the satisfaction of each party, they are carried over to the next interaction. If the child does what you ask but feels that she has "lost face" in doing so, she will carry power issues into the next interaction. With *power deficits*, the next interaction becomes even more important. The fight for power will be greater and the potential for this interaction to explode will be high.

Similarly, if the child does not feel heard, the need to be heard will be greater at the next meeting. **Each succeeding interaction will be more tense and potentially more explosive as power and expression issues are left unresolved. Deficits accumulate and are carried over to the next interaction.**

The child is not the only one with residual power and expression deficits. You, as the parent, can also have deficits that must be dealt with. That is why when I tell you to remain calm or to keep the Personal part of the relationship active, I don't mean that you should "swallow your feelings." When you are hurt or angry, if you do not deal with those feelings, you will carry over the deficits and you will be the one to escalate the next interaction.

Figure 8. *Unresolved power and expression issues escalate the interaction as irrationality takes over.*

It is okay to say, "That really makes me mad!" or "It really hurts me when you talk to me like that." After you make a statement like that, however, you should leave the room. Your statement should not be an implied demand that the child change his behavior. Such an implied demand will just get the child's defenses going again. The statement should simply be about what you are feeling, using an

"I-statement." In this way it is more difficult for the child to fight the demand (since there is none), and the statement will more likely be listened to. It will more likely have the effect you want it to have.

Power and expression deficits can also explain why sometimes one small word or even a certain look can "suddenly" launch people into a major fight. It is not the particular moment or the particular look or word that launched the conflict. The fight has been building, maybe without your awareness, for a long time. There is no easy fix at this point. The interaction has been developing into a major struggle because of power and expression deficits. At this point, it will take strategic interactional work to resolve the conflict and to keep further conflicts from erupting.

Irrationality

Look again at the argument with the child about cleaning up the room. Is the child's statement, "It's my room and I'll keep it any way I want to," a totally rational one? Is the "rationality" getting worse as she says, "Why don't you try and make me?" Have your children ever come up with really "lame" excuses and nonsense arguments during a disagreement?

- *"Everyone else is doing it."*
- *"There's no danger in doing that"* (jumping from a 100-foot bridge).
- *"If you let me have my allowance now, I'll never ask you for another thing."*
- *"I'm late because I forgot to look at my watch. That's not my fault."*
- *"If you would've bought me that pair of $150 jeans, I wouldn't feel bad about myself and I wouldn't have to act bad."*

You may have heard other irrational things coming from your child's mouth and gotten worried. "What's wrong with my child? She must be crazy. I'd better take her to therapy!" Yes, children do get quite irrational at times.

Parents can also get irrational. Have you ever said something (or done something) only to tell yourself the next day, "Why did I say that? I had promised myself I would never say that again. I know it doesn't do any good." The next day you may review one of these battles and even find yourself saying, "Oh, my gosh! I sounded just like my parent(s)!" Is this irrationality? Probably so.

Figure 9.
Irrationality is a product of negative interactions.

Though you realize that you, too, have been irrational, do you believe that you are normally an irrational person? Probably not. In the heat of escalating negative interactions, though, you do and say things you wouldn't normally do and say. Your child, likewise, is not inherently irrational. **In a negative interaction, irrational behavior comes out in both of you. Irrationality is a product of the interaction, not a permanent mental state.**

The lessons you have been teaching your child throughout her entire life have not been lost. They are in the child somewhere. She cannot act on them, though, in the midst of a negative interaction.

If irrationality is a product of negative interactions, you can increase *rationality* by improving the interaction. The high level of irrationality just shows you how important the power and expression issues have become and how influential the residual deficits are. It is so important to each of you to win the contest that both of you resort to irrational means (without being aware of it) to achieve your goals. By reducing the power and expression deficits, the need to win is also reduced.

Remember also that whatever you want your child to learn through an interaction will not be learned if she has resorted to irrationality. You can be making perfect sense and she can be completely "bonzo," but the child will never realize it in the irrational state. By interacting in such a way that irrationality is reduced and rationality is increased, you have a much better chance of getting your child to see the sense you are making and the nonsense she is making.

Points to Remember
from Chapter 2

1. The meaning of a message is in the interpretation given that message by the receiver.

2. Whenever you want something from someone, you are in the weaker position. All the other person has to do is *not do* it.

3. Power and expression issues are present in every interaction.

4. When the parent is expending *all* the energy, it is a sure sign that a power struggle is occurring.

5. Each succeeding interaction will be more tense and potentially more explosive as power and expression deficits are left unresolved.

6. Irrationality— a product of a negative interaction— can come out in both participants.

7. Reducing irrationality is the first goal of effective interactions.

8. Deficits operate as strongly in parents as they do in children.

We get convinced that the wall is hurting more than we are, as we are beating our heads against it.

—Howard Bad Hand,
Realities and Relationships Conference,
Taos Institute, NM (1993)

Chapter 3

What Do We Do About It?
The Six P's

If we get involved in interactions that end up as major power struggles that are negative for everyone involved, the solution is to get out of — and stay out of — those negative reciprocal interactions. That's the magic answer you've been waiting for.

Patient: Doc, my arm hurts when I do this.

Doctor: Then don't do that! That'll be $50.

The solution really is that simple — don't get into negative interactions. Yet staying out of negative interactions is very difficult, and all the work will have to come from you.

Why won't the child help you in this? The child is in the more powerful position. The child gets some sense of power, competence, and control from being in an interaction like this. Usually he does not consciously have these feelings. There is just some sense that this is an interaction over which he has some control. Remember that children have very little control in their lives. They have no choice about where they live, whom they live with, where they go to school, who their parents are, who their siblings are, how much money they have, what kind of work they can do, what subjects they take in school, and many other things.

Being in control of something is very attractive and comfortable. They don't necessarily want to be in control of their parents or their families, but they want to be in control of something. Sometimes interactions are the only things they have that they can control.

Because of this, they have little motivation to change. If you don't like the way the interactions go, it will be up to you to change them.

As hard as that fact is to face, it may be even harder to acknowledge that you, as well as your child, find some comfort in repeated negative interactions. They become habits. There are no surprises. Your child knows how the interactions go, and so do you. Your child knows that if he says such and such, you will react in such and such a way. You know that your child will probably react a certain way to certain requests or rules you make. **You may not be happy with your child's responses, but they are predictable.** The negative interactions get to be habits for both of you. Habits are comfortable because they are predictable.

Getting into negative interactions is also very normal. When your child invites you into a negative interaction by being angry, defying your authority, or breaking a rule, it is very natural for you to respond with anger, indignation, or more power. That is how we get into these kinds of interactions. They are the natural things to do. When we are attacked, we want to fight. If we are parents, we want to be in control and to "parent." There is nothing wrong or abnormal about getting into negative interactions. When we feel a deficit of power or when we don't feel heard, we work hard at correcting those deficits. If, however, acting in this normal manner is not getting you the results you want, it is time to do something different.

Doing Something Different

To change the interaction, you do something — anything — different (Figure 10). Doing something different is not easy because what you were doing felt natural. The different thing will be unnatural. The difference between what you have done before and the new thing may also be very subtle.

For example, parents often try to change their behavior while still retaining the need to have power. Their attempts at changing the interaction fail because, while what they say and do is different, it is still in the *category of "power."* The parent's new behaviors are still *power-based.* The child responds to this power play by continuing his own power play. Although the words may have changed, the interaction has not.

For instance, in order to change the interaction, some parents try to ignore their child when the child is yelling at them. They believe that this is different from engaging in a yelling match that they can't

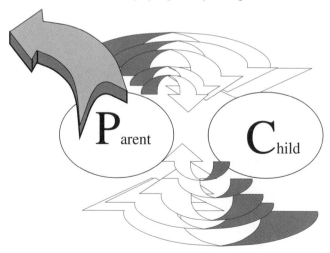

Figure 10. Negative interactions can be broken by doing something different.

win. And, of course, it is different. But how do you feel when someone ignores you? It often makes you want to yell louder to get the person back into the argument. Ignoring is a very powerful move. The child may even give up trying to talk to you, but the interaction has not really changed. Power is still at its base. The next interaction will start with the unresolved power issues and expression deficits from this interaction.

Be sure that you are changing what you are doing, not just disguising it. Change the base of power.

We have seen that doing something different is not as easy as it may seem. Outlined below are six steps you can follow to plan your moves and changes strategically. The six steps are the "Six P's of Parenting": *Prepare, Predict, Plan, Practice, PAT (Praise, Appreciate, and Thank), and Patience.*

When followed closely, and after much practice, the six P's will help you change your interactions with your child and thus change your relationship with your child.

Prepare

The outcome of any plan depends more on proper preparation than on anything else. Preparing in this case means that you should:

- know the power struggle cycle.

- know your "hooks."

- know your child's "hooks."

- know the symptoms of a power struggle.

The concept of the power struggle is not difficult. Keep it in mind and watch how it operates in all of your interactions and those you witness. Review Chapter 2 often. The more you think about it, the easier it is to recognize, and thus, avoid.

Hooks are the little behaviors (verbal and nonverbal) that get the power struggle started. Things that upset me and get me to defend and argue may not be the things that get you upset. It is important, then, that you know what your own hooks are. Hooks can be certain looks, a particular tone of voice, certain words, or particular actions. When you ask your child to do something and he gives you that look that says to you, "I'll do it, but I'm being unfairly treated to have to lift a finger around here!" is that what sets you off? Does that lead you into talking about his "attitude," which he then denies? Does that then lead you to talking about his "denying it," which leads to more denial? That one look can start a negative interaction unless you are aware of how it hooks you, and you learn to avoid it.

Figure 11. *How does your child "hook" you?*

Your child also has hooks. There are probably times when he is more likely to argue with you or refuse to do something. When he is in the middle of his favorite television program, he will probably be resentful of your request to take out the garbage. If your request is worded as a demand, you will most likely engage his *automatic defense system.* Be aware of when and how you interact with your child. If many of your interactions are not satisfactory, try changing the timing or wording of your requests since those may be "hooks" for your child.

Be aware of the symptoms of a power struggle. When both of you are screaming at the top of your lungs, it is pretty easy to realize that you are in a power struggle, but it is also too late to avoid all the negativity that comes with it. Be aware of the early signs:

- Do you feel that slight tension in your chest or neck?

- Are your voices beginning to rise?

- Do you feel your anger beginning to rise?

- Are you becoming frustrated?

- Can you sense anger or frustration in your child?

- Do you find yourself explaining a lot?

- Do you seem to be defending yourself?

Things to Do:

❑ Review Chapter 2.

❑ Make a list of all of your hooks and add to it as you become aware of new ones.

❑ Make a list of your child's hooks.

❑ Make a list of your early signs of being in a power struggle.

Predict

Most parents I talk with tell me that the problems they are having with their kids are not new ones. They have been happening for months, or even years. They say, "I've told her over and over again. She never listens. We seem to have the same argument all the time!" The repetition is very frustrating, and it can wear a parent down. However, there is a positive aspect to the repetition. It actually gives you an advantage. Because you have been through this argument so many times before, you can predict your child's actions and words. You can also predict your own actions and words. In fact, the whole situation has probably become some kind of tense, angry "dance" that you both know the steps to, and once the "music" starts, you both blindly, automatically go into the routine.

Being able to predict the steps allows you to change them. Becoming aware of the dance allows you to stop dancing.

Figure 12. *What are the signs that a power struggle is beginning? Can you predict what will happen next?*

Answer these questions:

❑ *How will your child react to this situation (based on your review of reactions in the past)?*

❑ *What will she say? How will she invite you into the dance?*

❑ *What hooks will there be?*

❑ *What is **your own** first step in the dance?*

Plan

When you have prepared yourself with knowledge about interactions and predicted how a situation may go, you are ready to **plan**. In other words, when you can "see" the interaction taking place—like a videotape in your head—*then* you are ready to *plan*. Plan to do something different. Make specific plans intentionally to change the next interaction.

❑ What will you say and do instead of what you normally say and do? The **Phrases for Strategic Interaction** (p. 41) are offered as a place to start. They are things you can say that help you stay out of the power struggle and give you time to think about your next response. The most important function of the phrases is that they do not encourage a negative interaction. They are neutral, not inflammatory.

❑ What is your game plan for staying out of the power struggle? Choose three phrases you are comfortable with.

❑ How will you continue to deal with your child's hooks?

❑ Which phrases will you memorize and use? They don't have to be something intelligent, philosophical, or important. They only have to avoid escalating the interaction. I often simply use "Wow."

Teenage client: "I'm going to join a gang and get my lip tattooed."

Strategic Interaction Phrases

Try using one of these time-tested phrases the next time you find yourself in a negative interaction:

❑ *"Wow!"*

❑ *"I never thought of it that way before."*

❑ *"I'm not sure I understand. Could you tell me some more about it?"*

❑ *"It seems that I've made you angry. What did I do?"*

❑ *"I know you're going to be [mad, disappointed, etc.], but the consequence to breaking the rule is [grounding, no telephone for two days, etc.]."*

❑ *"That's interesting!"*

❑ *"Come to me with an alternate plan."*

❑ *"I'm sorry."*

❑ *"What do you think about it?"*

❑ *"What do **you** think should happen?"*

❑ *"I'm going to have to think about that for awhile."*

❑ *"I can see why you'd be [mad, upset, sad, frustrated, etc.]."*

❑ *"I wish things could go better between us. Let me know if you have any ideas about how we can do that."*

❑ *"We seem to be at a standstill. Let's meet to talk about this again [a specific time in the future]."*

My response: "Wow!"

If I reacted the way my impulses told me to (e.g., "What? Are you crazy? That's dangerous and stupid!"), I would be risking putting the child in the position of defending his thoughts and actions. By responding simply with "Wow," I do not make him defensive, do not increase his irrationality, and so have a better chance of being able to have a meaningful, effective, and influential dialogue with him.

Figure 13. *How do you participate in the escalation of negative interactions?*

❑ Develop a game plane for staying out of power struggles. Understand that even though you use a phrase and initially avoid the power struggle, your child will probably immediately come back with another hook.

You have to be prepared for that one also. Choose three phrases you are comfortable with and practice.

Practice

Once you have your plan of action, **practice** it until it becomes a natural, automatic response. Enlist the aid of your friend or spouse. Have the other person play the role of your child. Practice some of the phrases and see how the other person responds.

❏ Is she less able to argue with you?

❏ Does he seem at a loss as to how to continue the argument?

❏ Does she feel "heard" and respected, or does she feel manipulated and overpowered?

❏ Are you in control of yourself and of the interaction, even if you are not in control of the child at this time?

Mentally practice while driving, exercising, cleaning house, returning phone calls. Verbally practice with friends. Even record yourself. Rehearsal is important for replacing old interactional patterns with new ones. Practice new ones until they feel comfortable.

PAT (Praise, Appreciate, and Thank)

As we talked about in Chapter 2, it is important to balance getting your child to cooperate (the Business side) with positive, warm, respectful interactions (the Personal side). A child who "loses face" will have a blow to her self-esteem and may feel angry enough to want to find a way to retaliate.

When the child does what you request, or even when the child makes improvement toward doing what is expected, you can say, "Thanks for straightening your room. I really appreciate that!" Even when you have to enforce a negative consequence, it can be done in a warm way. You can say, "Because you did not clean up your room as we had agreed, I'm afraid you'll have to be grounded on Friday. I wish that didn't have to happen. I know you wanted to go to that movie. Let me know if there is something we can do to get things done without having to resort to punishments." The Business side is always more impactful when accompanied by personal praise rather than control.

Patience

Finally, have patience! Changing how you interact is not easy. Even when you are successful, overnight cures are not guaranteed. Keep your eyes open for the changes, though. You may see that when you use strategic interactions, the child does not really know what to do. The child is accustomed to the power struggle that he knows he can ultimately win. When you refuse to play the game, though, the child is at a loss. Parents report noticing their children hesitating or groping for words to try to bring the parent back into the power struggle.

In severe situations, results may not come so soon. But every time you avoid the power struggle by using a Strategic Interaction, every time the interaction goes well, the chance of the next interaction going well will be greatly increased. Over time, the interactions become increasingly positive and productive. If nothing else, they become less stressful and you can enjoy your child more.

When parents avoid the traps set by their children, use Strategic Interaction phrases, and follow the **Parent's Creed** (p. 49), situations go smoother, more is accomplished, and feelings and relationships are more positive.

Remember:

"Relating" is a process that requires curiosity, collaboration, and mutual respect. It is not an inborn skill. It must be planned, and it must be practiced. It must be learned, and it can indeed be taught.

What Strategic Interaction Looks Like: A Brief Example

Let's take the situation we discussed earlier, in which the child draws the parent into a negative interaction over cleaning the room.

Parent: Please go clean up your room.

Child: Quit telling me what to do.

P (angrily): Don't take that tone of voice with me!

Do the Strategic Interaction phrases offer any help here? Consider, for instance, a slight change:

Parent: Please go clean up your room.

Child: Quit telling me what to do.

P (calmly, with concern): Wait. It seems I've made you angry. What did I do?

Imagine being in this interaction. How would you imagine the atmosphere in the second scenario as compared to the first? Do you think that the second example might be at least a little less tense? If the parent says the "phrase" with sincere concern and curiosity, she is inviting a dialogue rather than a power struggle. Already then, and very quickly, the interaction has changed.

Let's imagine how this could go on from here. To make it difficult, let's imagine that this is a child who is used to negative interactions and is good at drawing the parent in.

Parent: Wait. It seems that I've made you angry. What did I do?

Child: You're always trying to tell me what to do!

P: I'm sorry. I guess nobody likes being told what to do. I didn't realize I was doing it so much. I'll try to watch that in the future.

You may be saying, "What a wimp that parent is!" So far, the parent is getting nothing back for all the strategic interacting she is doing. But can you allow that at least they are not fighting at this point?

Remember how quickly the other interaction got ugly? At least at this point the atmosphere is calmer; there is no fighting, and nobody has had to resort to "irrationality" yet. Maybe, since this isn't going as the child expected so far, he is a bit off balance and a little unsure about where the interaction will go from here. He has to pay attention instead of tuning out and automatically falling into the negative interaction cycle. Also, since the parent seems to be listening to his concerns and feelings, the child is not fortifying his defenses. He feels better about this interaction in general.

Figure 14. *Try an alternative position that avoids the "power position."*

But let's go on with this imaginary interaction.

Parent: I'll try to watch that in the future.

Child: Yeah, right!

P: In the meantime, keeping your room straight was one of the things we had agreed on. You probably don't like nagging, and I don't either. Why don't you come to me with an alternate plan? Let's meet tomorrow at nine and we'll discuss it some more.

Well, what do you think now? They have stayed out of a fight. The parent has given very little to rebel against and has not been drawn into a negative interaction. The parent has maintained an attitude of respect toward the child and modeled calm, problem-solving skills. Under these conditions, if the history of interactions has not been too negative for too long, the chances of the two parties working out a mutually satisfactory solution are pretty good.

If there has been a long history of negative interactions, there is still a good chance of the two working out a solution. It just may take a little longer. The child has been used to defending against power and coming up with ways to be powerful. Power has been his whole experience with parents, and with adults in general.

When you do something different, the child doesn't know what it is. He's thinking, "Is this some sort of trick? What does she mean by 'Come to me with an alternate plan'? I'm not going to fall for that."

Trust, then, becomes the issue. The child may not believe that you are really getting out of the power role and into a more relational one. He will continue to try to pull you back into the old, negative interactions until he gains some trust that you are not using this as a power technique. For a little while he may continue to be the nasty little devil you've come to know. With patience, trust in this way of parenting, and vigilant awareness of your continued responses under this pressure, the interactions and the relationship will eventually change.

There are times when a relationship has gone so far that a child is in danger of ruining her life if there is no serious intervention. Sometimes children have to be placed away from home for a while. Even when things have gone this far, if the parents begin to make the changes I have talked about using Strategic Interaction principles, the possibility of recovery of the child and the relationship will be greatly enhanced. **It is never too late to begin to improve interactions.**

The Results

You will see immediate results from using Strategic Interaction. Parents report that when they truly are able to get out of negative interactions, they quickly notice significant changes. Things you may notice are:

- The tension between the parent and child is reduced, and a fight does not occur.

- The child seems at a loss. He really doesn't know what to say next.

- The child has a sort of confused look on his face as he tries to figure out what happened and what to do next.

- Instead of the parent pursuing the child trying to get him to change while the child flees, suddenly the child is pursuing the parent, trying to get the parent back into the weaker position in the negative interaction.

- The power is suddenly switched to the parent.

- The parent expends less energy while the child expends more.

These changes are the beginning of the end of the problems. The shift from trying to control the child to controlling the interaction will lead to changes in *behavior* and *attitude*. There may be a brief escalation of the unwanted behavior as the child attempts to regain power and control. As the parent continues interacting strategically, however, the child is forced to think and behave more rationally, responsibly, and cooperatively.

> *It is much easier to manage the interaction than it is to control the child.*

The Parent's Creed

As a parent who uses Strategic Interaction:

1. I will keep the Business and Personal sides of my relationship *separate*.

2. I will use as much of the Personal side as possible.

3. I will *adopt a position* where positive interaction is more likely.

4. I will keep positions *flexible*.

5. I will *avoid blaming* the child.

6. I will remain as *calm as possible*.

7. I will *"hear"* my child's thoughts and feelings.

8. I will remain *rational*.

9. I will *promote rationality* in my child.

10. I will avoid:

    a. reacting defensively.

    b. giving long explanations.

    c. trying to get my child to "understand."

    d. trying to give my child "insights."

    e. convincing my child that I'm being "fair."

    f. trying to change my child.

The Beginning of the End of the Problems

Immediate Changes as a Result of Strategic Interactions

❏ The **tension** between the parent and child is **reduced**, and a fight does not occur.

❏ The **child seems at a loss**. He really doesn't know what to say next.

❏ The **child has a sort of confused look** on his face as he tries to figure out what happened and what to do next.

❏ Instead of the **parent pursuing the child** and trying to get him to change while the child flees, suddenly the **child is pursuing the parent,** trying to get the parent back into the weaker position in the negative interaction.

❏ The **power** is suddenly **switched** to the parent.

❏ The parent expends less energy while the child expends more.

Points to Remember from Chapter 3

THE SIX P'S OF STRATEGIC INTERACTION

1. Prepare by knowing your own "hooks."

2. Predict your child's response.

3. Plan to use "strategic interaction phrases."

4. Practice. And practice some more.

5. PAT (Praise, Appreciate, and Thank).

6. Patience.

He who establishes his argument by noise and command shows that his reason is weak.

—Michel de Montaigne

Who holds a power but newly gained is ever stern of mood.

—Aeschylus

Chapter 4

Positions and Other Important Things

Parents often deal with children from a position of *power* or *authority*. When interactions and relationships are not going well, it may be that this position is feeding the negative interaction and making it easy for the child to battle you. If this is the case, it is time to try a different *position*. Taking a different position is not easy until you practice it, but it will clearly give you an interactional advantage.

The power or authority position has actually made you weak and helpless against the rebelliousness that your position has encouraged. Taking any other position will change the interaction. In the alternative positions, you have choices. In a power position, you can only "do power." Power is not helping you right now. In fact, it is hurting you.

Remember, the solution to the dilemma with many kids is to *do something different*. You can't do something different if you stay in the same position.

Some examples of different positions are:

❏ *Curious*	❏ *Concerned*
❏ *Calm*	❏ *Helpful*
❏ *Apologetic*	❏ *Accepting*
❏ *Listening*	❏ *Caring*
❏ *Weak*	❏ *Collaborative*

This list of alternative positions is not exhaustive. You may think of others. When you get into negative interactions, any position that is different from the position you are in is a useful one. Adopting any of these positions minimizes the chances of getting into power struggles. All the positions stress the *Personal* side of the relationship rather than the Business, but none of them demands that you give up the *Business* side. You can compromise on the Business, *but you must always include it*. Note, however, that the tendency is to give up the Personal side. These positions help you keep both sides involved in your relationship.

❏   *Curious.* When your child refuses a request, it will be hard for him to get into an argument with you if you are genuinely curious about why. Examples of phrases in this position are:

"I'm not sure I understand. Could you tell me some more about it?"

"It seems that I've made you angry. What was it that I did?"

A word of caution about the curious position. "Why" questions can be experienced as blaming if the tone of voice and facial expression don't show genuine curiosity. Be clear in your own mind, even if you are pretending for now, that you really are curious at this step.

❏   *Calm.* Since anger is often a part of power and since your child can easily draw you into anger, staying calm provides a very different reaction from what your child may have been expecting. Your anger probably helps escalate your child's anger, so your calmness should keep the interaction less tense and more rational. Examples of phrases in this position are:

"Wow!"

"We seem to be at a standstill. Let's meet to talk about this again [some specific time in the future]."

Performing vs. Taking a Position

Remember that the meaning of a message depends on how the receiver of the message interprets it. The same dynamics apply to positions. You may intend to adopt a curious or listening position, but your child may still see you in a powerful role. You cannot *take* a position and assume that your child will see you in it. You have to *act* or *perform* the position. That means that you have to say and do things that demonstrate you are operating from that position and not some other one. The position is defined by what you say and do, not by what you intend.

Initially, your child may not trust that you are changing your position and your interaction. He will be watching for what you do next. When you have shown him that you are acting in a different way, he can learn to trust that.

❏ *Apologetic.* Authority figures never apologize. They try to force others to think they are right, thereby encouraging the other to think of more and better reasons why the authority is actually wrong. Apologizing can keep the child from having to rationalize his mistakes and having to spend so much energy proving you wrong. It also models "ownership" of one's own behaviors. Examples of phrases in this position are:

"I can see why you'd be [mad, upset, sad, frustrated, etc.]."

"I'm sorry."

❏ **Listening.** Remember that expression is also a part of every interaction. If you don't listen, you can't hear what your child may be trying to tell you. He may have to try harder and harder, continuing the negative interaction until you do listen. Examples of phrases in this position are:

"I never thought of it that way before."

"That's interesting!"

❏ **Weak.** Being weak is certainly the opposite of being powerful. You can't say powerful things which invite powerful opposition when you are in a weak position. You almost have to listen and be calm, curious, and apologetic in a weak position. It is a very hard position for parents to take, but sometimes it can be the beginning of turning negative interactions into positive ones. Adopting a weak position often allows the parent to get out of the negative cycle and do something different. Examples of phrases in this position are:

"I wish things could go better between us. Let me know if you have any ideas about how we can do that."

*"You're too big for me to **make** you do the lawn, but I hope we can come to some agreement about it."*

❏ **Concerned.** When the child expects you to be mad and/or authoritarian, it is quite a shock when, instead, you are concerned. If he expects you to be mad, he may come into the interaction defensive and angry. Since you can't get anywhere with him when he is in this position, you are helping your cause by taking a different position from what he is expecting. Examples of phrases in this position are:

"It seems that I've made you angry. What was it that I did?"

"I can see why you'd be [mad, upset, sad, frustrated, etc.]."

❏ *Helpful*. Offering help models calmness, generosity, and collaboration. It gives the message, "I am not a tyrant, but things must get done. What can I do to help you get it done?" Examples of phrases in this position are:

> *"It seems that I've made you angry. What was it that I did?"*

> *"I wish things could go better between us. Let me know if you have any ideas about how we can do that."*

❏ *Accepting*. You would be surprised at what a powerful move it is to accept the thoughts and feelings of someone. It is the opposite of arguing with him. That doesn't mean that you *agree with* him, or that you have to go along with his point of view. It simply means that you're willing to entertain the idea and that maybe you can see the logic in it even if you don't agree with it. Examples of phrases in this position are:

> *"I'm going to have to think about that for awhile."*

> *"I never thought of it that way before."*

❏ *Caring*. It is again surprising to a child when, instead of being angry, you ask about how she is. She is knocked off balance. She expects one thing; you do a different, Personal thing. Examples of phrases in this position are:

> *"I wish things could go better between us. Let me know if you have any ideas about how we can do that."*

> *"I can see why you'd be [mad, upset, sad, frustrated, etc.]."*

❏ *Collaborative*. The position that you want for both you and your child is collaborative. Here, instead of arguing and fighting against each other, you find ways to work out your differences and work together. You have to model that kind of behavior for your child in order for her to learn it. It may not be possible to be collaborative about everything, but the more you can get in a "we" position, the less stress you will have. Examples of phrases in this position are:

> *"We seem to be at a standstill. Let's meet to talk about this again [some specific time in the future]."*

"Come to me with an alternate plan."

"I wish things could go better between us. Let me know if you have any ideas about how we can do that."

You may notice that some of the phrases are used in more than one position. There are no exact phrases for each position. The main point is that you get out of power struggles originating from the power/authority position, by getting out of that position. Again, the list of phrases is not exhaustive. They are only a place to start. Find some you like, and practice and experiment with them.

Flexibility

Flexibility is important in any interaction. A power position is not necessarily a bad thing. **When what you are doing is not working, however, you should be able to change to another position.** For instance, a curious position is also not always the best one to be in. Many times it is better simply to listen (i.e., take a listening position) than to ask questions..

It takes great skill and practice to be able to move from one position to another as the need develops in the interaction. Continue to pay attention to how your child is responding to the position you are trying to be in, keeping a flexible mindset. Change positions as necessary.

To help you see how this works in action, Chapter 5 provides an example of dealing with a child who doesn't want to clean his room. I have included notations of what position the parent may be coming from with each step in the interactions that follow.

Make an Effort to Enjoy Your Child

When a parent has gotten to the point where she is almost always in negative interactions with her child, there seems to be constant tension between them. They are always mad at each other. Since they are in a battle for power, they can never let their guards down for fear of losing the battle. Neither can enjoy the other. Gone is the positive, *Personal* side of the relationship.

An important part of changing the interaction, then, is to reintroduce some of the enjoyment that may have been present in the past. It can be very hard for a parent to find something she enjoys about her child in the midst of the negative interaction cycle. It may take much creativity on the part of the parent to find ways to enjoy the child. *Enjoying the child, or at least trying to, is another way to change the interaction.* The message is, "I'm giving up the power struggle. I want to have a good relationship with you, not a domineering one." Being friendly to the child, even after or during some of the tense moments, is a strong sign that the parent is making an important shift in interaction.

The more the parent stays out of negative interactions, the easier it is to be more positive. At first, though, it takes a conscious effort. Here are some suggestions for how to begin an enjoyable relationship again:

❏ *Talk about something the child likes to talk about* (e.g., football, music, hair styles, clothes). Remember just to listen. Get to know your child.

❏ *Offer an enjoyable activity.* Don't think of it as "giving in" or bribery. Just think of it as an enjoyable family outing.

❏ *Force yourself to make a positive remark to your child.* Does your child have a sense of humor? Is she energetic? Is she resourceful? Is she observant? Is she trendy? Is she good at fighting trends? Is she bravely experimental? Is she friendly or does she seem to be easily liked? Is she loyal? Is she creative? Is she strong-minded or independent?

Even in some of the "bad" things the child does, the seed of a positive trait may exist. The creative parent may be able to find this tiny seed and nurture it by making a positive statement about it at the appropriate time.

❏ *Mention happy remembrances you have of the child.*
"Remember that time we all went to [Disneyland,
South Dakota, the mall]? I really enjoyed that." There
is no need to say more. Just that positive memory will
be a powerful message.

❏ *Be aware of feelings you have about your present
negative relationship besides anger, frustration, and
disappointment.* Do you miss the enjoyable times, the
close feelings you once had? Tell your child. "I miss
going fishing with you." "We hardly ever talk anymore. I miss knowing you." After making these statements, leave the room. You don't want your child to
feel burdened by these remarks. If the child feels you
are expecting something from him after you say these
things, he will not react well. If you make such a
remark and show him he doesn't have to do anything
about it, he may take it as a sign that underneath the
tension of the negative interactions, you still love
him, that there is more to your relationship than the
negative part.

Doing any of the above is **different** from being in a struggle.
Doing something different is a step in the direction of change.

Points to Remember
from Chapter 4

1. Only when you change positions can you have options.

2. When you get into negative interactions, any position that is different from the position you are in is a useful one.

3. The position that you want for both you and your child is collaborative. Instead of arguing and fighting with each other, you find ways to work out your differences and work together.

4. Make an effort to enjoy your child.

Lawful and settled authority is very seldom resisted when it is well employed.

—Samuel Johnson (1750)

Calvin and Hobbes
by Bill Watterson

Reprinted by permission of Universal Press Syndicate.

Chapter 5

Strategic Interaction in Action:

"What Do I Do When My Child Won't Do Chores?"

In this chapter, I will elaborate on a model for understanding why kids sometimes won't cooperate and how you, as the parent, can handle the situation. I will illustrate by exploring the problem of *children not doing chores.* It is intended to give further understanding of Strategic Interaction in general, as well as specifics about this particular problem.

Please remember that the exact words and phrases used in the following examples are less important than the concepts. It is the general philosophy, flow, and rhythm of Strategic Interaction that you want to learn. Try practicing Strategic Interaction by examining what this child says to hook the parent into a negative interaction, and then try thinking up alternative responses. Think about what position the parent is taking that is getting him into trouble. Be aware of what the parent is wanting from the child that allows the child simply to refuse. This can be very subtle. *Whenever there is a problem interaction, one person is requesting something from the other.*

Getting the Bedroom Cleaned

Now let's go back to the original example we used earlier about the child cleaning up the room. Let's say that we know that the child has become quickly angry and defensive about this issue in the past, thus the parent decides to take a different approach from the start. Unless otherwise noted, all of the statements from the parent can be considered to be from the Personal side of the relationship. (Also, in the parentheses, I have indicated the position reflected by the phrase.)

Parent: Hey, I was wondering if you could clean up your room.

Child: No, I can't.

P: Oh. [Pause] How come? (Curious)

C: *Because I don't feel like it.*

P: *Oh, I'm sorry you don't feel good. Are you OK? (Concerned)*

C: *Yeah, I'm fine. I just don't feel like cleaning up my room right now.*

P: *Later then?*

C: *Yeah. Later.*

P: *Let me know if there's anything I can do for you. (Helpful)*

C: *OK.*

At this point the parent leaves.

Now, again the room didn't get cleaned up, right? However, a fight did not happen and the child did not lose face or have to resort to much irrationality. The parent has presented himself as calm, understanding, and willing to listen and help. Depending on what happens next, this is a pretty good position for the parent to be in. He certainly hasn't given up power by giving the child much to fight about.

Let's pretend that the first part of that conversation took place sometime in the afternoon. Now it is 8:00 p.m. the same day:

Parent: I noticed that your room still isn't picked up. Are you OK? (Concerned)

Child: Yeah.

P: *Well, the room being cleaned up was something we had agreed on as part of what you would do to help out. [Business side] How can we get that to happen better? (Collaborative)*

C: *I don't know.*

P: *Well, could you think about it? I don't want it to become a problem between us. (Caring; Business side) We'll get together tomorrow morning, OK?*

C: *OK.*

End of that discussion.

Now the parent is putting a little more pressure on the child, but still not getting into a powerful role. He is still curious, concerned and listening. He is relying on their agreement about the room, rather than on his authority, as the basis of the request. He has asked the child to think about it without *demanding* that the child think about it, so the child will probably find it hard not to think about it, at least periodically.

Next morning:

Parent: Well, have you come up with anything?

Child: No.

P: Anything I can do to help? (Helpful, but not giving up on the Business Side)

C: No.

Still later, maybe the next day around noon:

P: Well, what have you come up with?

C (resigned or exasperated): I'll do the room.

P: Great! Thank you! (the PAT of the six P's)

Child cleans the room.

Okay, but what if the child still doesn't clean the room? Maybe the child was just lying to the parent to get the parent off his back.

Parent: Whoa! I thought you said you were going to do your room! What happened? (Curious).

Child: I guess I forgot.

P: Oh. Well, I have to tell you, I'm quite disappointed. Remember, we had agreed that if you don't do the chores we had outlined, you would [be grounded on a Friday night, lose your allowance for this week, have to go to bed an hour earlier, not go to the movies with us.] (Choose one. Make sure the consequence is one to which the child responds). *I guess that will have to happen. (Business side) I'm sorry. (Caring; Apologetic)*

Punishment in the form of a consequence was used in this case because the child did not cooperate, but the parent continued to keep a different attitude and position than that of power or authority. By doing this, he has reduced the tension, reduced the possibility of rebellion and irrationality, and has set it up for the child to cooperate next time.

Why might the child cooperate next time? Because there is not much for him to fight with. The parent has been nice all along, even apologizing for having to enforce the consequence. He has kept his cool and has, at all times, given the child options and has tried to involve the child in solving this problem. It is a difficult position to fight against.

Some kids will, of course, fight against even this position. A child who still wants to fight has probably been in lots of intense negative interactions. This may be the first time there has been something different. Even the very recalcitrant child will eventually respond to an interaction such as the one described above. It may take some time to begin to trust this new way of interacting. The parent will have to be aware of that and be willing to continue interacting *strategically* throughout the "trial" period.

If you have been in many negative interactions with your child, so that almost everything you do with him turns into a problem, it is important that you begin to turn these interactions around with Strategic Interaction principles. *The interaction is what is important right now, not the immediate result.*

You have to get used to dealing with your child in a different way, giving up the power position while regaining control over yourself and the situation. Your child has to get used to your being different. He has to come to trust that you are not trying to overpower him anymore and has to believe that what you are doing now is not a trick in the power play. With a very difficult child, this may take some *time . . .* and *patience.*

While the two of you are making these changes, rooms may not get cleaned up. The interaction around the room-cleaning contributes to the overall changes you are making. It is important that the interaction around a particular issue happens regardless of whether or not the child ends up cooperating at this time. The interaction is part of the positive change.

If you are in a real "war" with your child, be sure to pick your "battles" carefully. Is the room very important to you? If it is, then do what you have to do to be comfortable. Is the room a battle that you can lose if it helps you win the war? Maybe you can reassure yourself by thinking that even though the room did not get cleaned, you performed marvelously and have begun to change your relationship with your child.

Examine within yourself what you want from your child and why. Examine the things about which you really are adamant and that get you into negative interactions with your child. Can you alter them in any way, at least until you are having better interactions? *Remember that when you want something from your child, you are in a weak position — and the more intense your desire for that thing, the weaker you are.* Some things you want very badly may have to be set aside in order to improve your position in the interaction. It won't be productive to launch into a power-based interaction just because you wanted something from your child and became uncomfortable with that "weak position."

The following chapters will address other common problems that parents have with children. A way of understanding the problem from an interactional perspective will be presented, followed by an example of how a Strategic Interaction may help solve the problem, or at least set the stage for the problem's resolution.

Points to Remember
from Chapter 5

1. Using the Personal side and staying out of the power position does not mean that you give up the Business side of the relationship.

2. To keep your child from fighting with you, take a position that is hard to fight against.

3. When there has been a long history of negative interactions, changing the interaction and not the behavior is what is important now.

4. Both you and your child have to get used to dealing with each other in a different way.

5. At first, your child may think your difference is just another attempt at overpowering him.

6. Pick your battles carefully.

Children need models rather than critics.

—Joseph Joubert, *Pensees* (1842)

You can't teach cooperation by modeling domination.

—Jamie Raser
Effective Parenting Workshop
(1994)

Section 2

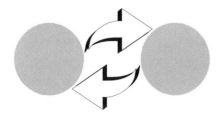

WHAT DO I DO WHEN . . . ?

Each chapter in this section addresses a different problem that parents run into with their children. All children are different. All parents are different. All families are different, and no situation is exactly the same as another. This section is meant as a guide to deal with the problem and the child in a way that is more likely to bring out the positive. The sample Strategic Interactions should be used only as starting places. The strategy you select may have to be modified to fit your unique situation.

Remember, if your parenting strategy is working well, keep doing what you're doing. However, **if it does not seem to be working, try something else.**

It is best to read all of the chapters to become very familiar with the subtleties of Strategic Interaction. Most situations are a combination of several different kinds of negative interactions. Therefore, when a particular problem emerges, consulting several pertinent chapters will give you ideas on how to use Strategic Interaction effectively.

For example, if the problem you face involves "obeying rules," it may be helpful to review the chapters on blaming others (Chapter 8), irresponsibility (Chapter 9,) and failing to complete chores (Chapter 5) in addition to the chapter on obeying rules (Chapter 15). They may all give insight into the problem and provide practical suggestions on how to proceed. Combining the suggestions in each of those chapters may be necessary. You may also want to reread some portions from Section 1 (especially the subsections on

"Flexibility" and "Doing Something Different") and then practice with someone.

The Strategic Interaction approach is not haphazard, and it is not particularly easy. The examples in Section 2 demonstrate how Strategic Interaction phrases and positions can be memorized, rehearsed, and then creatively applied to a variety of common parent-child struggles.

)

A question ain't really a question that you know the answer to.

—John Prine

Chapter 6

What Do I Do When. . .

. . . My Child Lies?

We can all think of reasons why children tell lies. They are often the same reasons why adults tell lies. Children often tell lies to cover for something they do, or something they want to do, that they aren't supposed to do.

Lying is often a result of:

• *a negative interaction,*

• *an ongoing negative relationship, or*

• *the expectation of a future negative interaction.*

Power and expression issues often have been left unresolved in previous interactions, so lying seems to the child to be the best way to avoid those deficits in the future. Lying can be diminished to a great extent, then, by handling interactions in a more positive way.

Upon discovering that a child has lied, some parents do something like this:

Parent: So, how was it at Beth's?

Child: Oh, fine.

P: Oh, really! Well, I just found out that you weren't at Beth's! Why did you lie to me? You're in big trouble now.

The Interactional Dynamics

The parent has made two mistakes here. First, she has played the "Gotcha Game." It is a game of power and may encourage the child to respond with power. One of the child's power moves could be to tell an irrational tale (a lie) and stick to it because to do otherwise would be letting the parent win the "Gotcha Game." The parent has inadvertently invited the child to try to outsmart her the next time and has encouraged her to lie again, only better.

The second mistake is asking why the child lied. Is there really an acceptable answer? The question implies that there is. The child is then encouraged to try to think up what an acceptable answer might be, and so is again encouraged to lie in this interaction. After the child has tried this and failed a few times, and since there really is no good answer, she will usually respond to that question with silence. Worse, though, is that the child learns not to trust when the parent asks a question. She learns that the parent is not really interested in the answer and that the parent may be setting her up with another form of the "Gotcha Game."

A Strategic Interaction

> *Parent: It seems that you weren't telling the truth when you said you were going to spend the night at Beth's. I found out that you were somewhere else.*

> *Child: How did you find out?*

> *P: Parents often find out things like that. The point is that I'm very disappointed that I can't trust you like I thought I could. I'm also very angry.*

> *C: Well, I'm sorry. I won't do it again.*

> *P: I hope you don't, but you have done it before. We had agreed that if you lied again, you would be grounded for the next two weekends, and that's what's going to happen.*

You may ask, "What if a child lies about everything, even when there is no need to?" For example:

> *Parent: I've been noticing that many times what you say turns out not to be true. It really makes me wonder if I can believe anything you say anymore. I don't like feeling that I can't trust you or trust what you say. Is there anything wrong?*

> *Child: No.*

*P: OK. Good. Have you noticed that you are telling more things
that don't seem to be true?*

C: No.

*P: OK, from now on I'll bring it up when what you are saying
doesn't seem to be true. I'll bring it to your attention and we
can check it out. OK?*

C: OK.

Even though the child may be on the defensive about her lying,
she knows that the parent will be watching out for it, so she may be
motivated to stop it. In this case, the parent has set it up to talk to the
child about the lying without blaming the child, accusing the child
or putting her on the defensive against the parent.

If the lies continue anyway, seemingly for no reason and reflect-
ing a strange sort of fantasy life, a consultation with a mental health
professional may be in order.

Things to Think About When Your Child Lies

❏ Don't play the "Gotcha Game."

❏ Asking why the child has lied gets you nowhere. It's
better to say, "I know that isn't the truth, and the consequence of telling a lie is . . . ."

❏ Proving the lie and then getting the child to admit to
it means that all the energy is coming from you. You
want to be in a position where the child has to spend
energy proving that it isn't a lie. He will tire of that
quickly.

In other words, carefully consider the evidence and
act on the evidence rather than on your child's story.
To avoid consequences, your child will have to be
sure the evidence changes. He can't change the evidence by just talking.

My words are but a whisper;
your deafness, a shout.

—Ian Anderson,
Thick as a Brick (1972)

Chapter 7

What Do I Do When. . .

. . . My Child Won't Communicate?

The task of adolescence is to achieve a sense of identity and independence. To do this, there must be some separation between teens and their parents and family. That's one reason adolescents don't share everything with you anymore.

A second reason is that they are involved in a different culture than you are. Teen culture has different values, tastes, sense of humor, and ideals from a parent's. Adolescents don't see things your way, and you don't see things their way. That makes it hard to have something in common to talk about. A third reason why communication may be difficult has to do with the **interactional dynamics.**

The Interactional Dynamics

Parent: Hey! You're spending entirely too much time in your room. We want you in here with us for a change.

Child: Oh, leave me alone.

P: What's the matter with you? You never talk to us anymore.

C: There's nothing wrong! I just don't have anything to say.

P: Well, you sure seem to have plenty to say to your friends on the telephone.

C: So what?

P: So, from now on, if you don't talk to us, you don't talk on the telephone.

C: OK! Fine! What do you want me to say?

P: Well, how was your day in school?

C: It sucked! Now, are you happy? I'll be in my room.

In the above example, the parent wanted to hear from the child so much that she resorted to forcing communication. That obviously didn't work very well. I once spoke with a parent who was very concerned about his son. The boy basically locked himself in his bedroom whenever he was home. He did not come out to eat meals with the family or participate in other family activities, so the parents knew very little about what was going on with the boy. They worried a lot.

The father decided that if only the boy would come to the dinner table for dinner with the family, they could worry less. Threatening punishment didn't seem to work, so the father began a nightly ritual of pleading with his son for 10 to 20 minutes at dinner time, through the boy's locked door. Of course, this also did not work.

I suggested that the father simply knock on the boy's door at dinner time and say, "Five minutes to dinner." He was then to leave. The first two nights the father did this, there was no response. On the third night, though, the father was amazed to see his son come to the dinner table. When the father got out of the negative interaction around dinner and reduced his desire for the boy to conform to his wishes, the negative interaction was ended and the boy was free to come out of his room.

Figure 15. *Forcing communication does not foster communication.*

Although teens are trying to become independent, they do want someone to talk with. That's why talking to their friends is so important to them. That's why they also may become attached to someone else's parent and enjoy sharing things with that person. Growing up is a scary thing. Adolescents actually would love to be able to talk about their fears and new experiences with someone they trust. They would love to trust you and talk to you about it. They want someone who will talk *with* them, not talk *at* them.

However, parents are too quick to get alarmed about what they hear from their children and tend to lecture, scold, and point out what's wrong with what they are hearing from their kids. That doesn't make for a very pleasant conversation from the child's standpoint.

The child gets the idea that when you say you want to hear from him, you actually mean that you *only want to hear what you want to hear* and not what is actually on the child's mind. If you really want to talk with your child, you have to be ready to hear things that may be hard to hear. And you have to be able to talk with your child about those things without making the child feel guilty, stupid, or immature. That means exploring with him how he feels, what he thinks, and how he plans to act about the subject. The child wants your advice, but first the child wants you to hear and respect what he thinks about the matter.

A Strategic Interaction

Parent: Hey, how's it going?

Child: Fine.

P: Good. How's school lately?

C: Fine.

P: Great! I know you were having a little trouble with math last semester. Is that still a problem for you?

C: That teacher sucks!

P: No kidding? What's up with him?

C: I don't know. He's got it in for me.

P: Uh oh! That can make things pretty rough.

C: Tell me about it! He gets so picky about the tiniest things, like if our homework's a little late. Big deal! The other teachers don't care.

P: Wow. What are you going to do?

C: I don't know. I may have to stay after school and take some tutoring with him. He gets real impressed with stuff like that.

> *P: Maybe that will work. Sounds like a good plan, anyway. Let me know how it goes, OK? And let me know if there's anything I can do to help.*
>
> *C: Sure. Thanks.*

This parent probably didn't like everything she heard from the boy, but she did hear about some things going on in the boy's life and set it up to hear more by asking to be filled in later. More importantly, though, by taking a position of sincere, noninterfering interest, she has shown the boy that she can be trusted to listen respectfully and unobtrusively. This boy will probably feel it is safe to share other things with this parent on down the road.

Things to Think About When Your Child Won't Communicate

❏ The task of adolescence is to achieve a sense of identity, independence, and self-agency.

❏ An adolescent can be viewed as a person from a different culture.

❏ Forcing communication does not foster communication.

❏ Teens want and need to talk to others about their thoughts and experiences. That is why their peers are so important to them. Peers may be the only ones who listen to them seriously.

❏ Parents tend to get alarmed at what they hear and start to lecture rather than listen.

❏ The child wants you to hear and respect him, and then offer your ideas.

❏ True power comes by listening first, rather than by lecturing first.

Calvin and Hobbes

by Bill Watterson

NOTHING I DO IS MY FAULT.

MY FAMILY IS DYSFUNCTIONAL AND MY PARENTS WON'T EMPOWER ME! CONSEQUENTLY, I'M NOT SELF-ACTUALIZED!

MY BEHAVIOR IS ADDICTIVE FUNCTIONING IN A DISEASE PROCESS OF TOXIC CODEPENDENCY.' I NEED HOLISTIC HEALING AND WELLNESS BEFORE I'LL ACCEPT ANY RESPONSIBILITY FOR MY ACTIONS!

ONE OF US NEEDS TO STICK HIS HEAD IN A BUCKET OF ICE WATER.

I LOVE THE CULTURE OF VICTIMHOOD.

Chapter 8

What Do I Do When. . .

. . . My Child Always Blames Others?

Blaming others is one way of refusing to accept personal responsibility.

Parent: What do you mean you got suspended today?!

Child: It wasn't my fault! Jimmy pushed me, so I pushed him back. The stupid principal didn't do anything to Jimmy, but he started it.

P: Don't talk that way about the principal! And I'm sure Jimmy would have gotten in trouble if he really did something. This is the third time this year that you've gotten into trouble for something like this.

C: *The kids always pick on me, and the teachers hate me.*
   They're all trying to get rid of me.

P: *If you'd act right, the teachers would treat you right.*

C: *I do act right. They just don't like me. When I do act right,*
   they still pick on me and blame me for everything anyway.

Figure 16. *Don't enter into an argument about*
who's to blame. Ask what the child will do to correct
the situation.

The Interactional Dynamics

The parent in this example would clearly like this child to admit
that he is doing something wrong so he can realize his mistake and
not repeat it. That is obviously not happening. The child sticks with,
and gets even more immersed in, a story about how he is *mistreated*.
He never has to see that he could change his behavior. Not accepting

responsibility and blaming others is a little like lying. It is a useful way to sidestep blame and trouble. Actually, it doesn't avoid trouble, but it can help a person avoid guilt about the trouble.

Trying to get a child to admit he is wrong inevitably involves trying to get him to accept guilt. *Guilt is painful.* It is the same, then, as trying to get him to accept pain. Admitting guilt often leads to punishment anyway, so why shouldn't a child try to avoid the pain and punishment if at all possible? Kids are geniuses at avoidance.

The parent is saying, "Admit you are wrong." The child is saying, "No." The child is saying, "Believe my excuse." The parent is saying, "No." This will go on and on.

A Strategic Interaction

Parent: You got suspended today?

Child: Yeah, but it wasn't my fault. Jimmy pushed me, so I pushed him back.

P: Then what happened?

C: The stupid principal saw me and I got in trouble. Nothing happened to Jimmy, and he started it.

P: (Shaking head in disbelief): Suspended again. That's the third time this year! What are we going to do about this?

C: I don't know. The kids pick on me, and the teachers don't like me. That's why I always get in trouble.

P: Why do you think the teachers don't like you?

C: I don't know. They think I'm a troublemaker.

P: That must be a hard thing to live down.

C: It is! No matter what happens, I get blamed for it.

P: What can you do about that?

C: Nothing! You can't change someone's mind.

P: I guess it's going to be rough on you then.

C: Yeah. Why don't you put me in another school?

P: I can't do that. I can't afford it. I wish I could. How are you going to last the rest of this year?

C: I don't know. I'm going to have to be real careful about what I do. I can't let Jimmy or anybody else get me in trouble anymore.

P: That may be hard to do. They've been pretty good at getting you into trouble up to now.

C: I know, but I'm not going to let them do it anymore.

P: Do you have a plan?

C: I'm just going to be cool.

P: OK. Let me know if I can help.

This parent avoided trying to get the child to take responsibility, so the child did not build up defenses in that direction. A shift began when the parent asked, "What are we going to do about this?" instead of "You'd better stop this." The parent also "heard" the child's complaints about unfairness so the child did not have to belabor that point either.

By the end, the child did not say, "I see now that it's all my fault and now I will try to improve my behavior." However, he was willing to do something different that implied that his behavior was a part of the problem. If he really could change his behavior in the way he planned, he would probably not get in as much trouble. He could then lose the troublemaker reputation and not get picked on as much. It wouldn't matter if he ever accepted responsibility for his behavior as long as he ended up changing his behavior in the right direction.

Things to Think About When Your Child Blames Others

❑ When children blame, listen first.

❑ It doesn't matter who is to blame—that is a red herring. The point is that the child either got in trouble or something negative happened.

❑ The first direction of change should be toward changing the behavior so that the incident doesn't happen again rather than trying to get the child to accept blame for it.

❑ The parent should bypass the "Who's to blame?" question and go to "What are you going to do about it and how can I help?"

❑ Don't get children to *admit fault.* Get them to *take responsibility*—which means taking responsible *action.*

Calvin and Hobbes

Reprinted by permission of Universal Press Syndicate.

Chapter 9

What Do I Do When. . .

. . . My Child Is Careless and Irresponsible?

Irresponsibility can take the form of not doing chores (see Chapter 5 on chores). It can also take the form of smaller things that prove to be very annoying to parents. For instance, typical "irresponsible" behaviors include not taking out the garbage when it is obviously full, leaving dishes all over the house, not telling the parent about an object needed for school until five minutes before school starts, not writing notes about where she is going, not calling to tell you she is there, not putting gas in the car, waiting until the last minute for everything. The list can go on and on.

The Interactional Dynamics

The parent's tendency is to get angry and blame. This, in turn, creates defensiveness in the child. The defensiveness brings out all the irrational excuses, blaming, and lies that we have already dealt with.

> *Parent: How many times have I told you about those dishes? You leave them in your room and they get dried, rotten food all over them. I'm sick and tired of cleaning up after you!*
>
> *Child: Fine. Don't then! I don't care.*
>
> *P: How can you stand all that garbage in your room?*
>
> *C: I don't care.*
>
> *P: You may not care, but I do!*
>
> *C: I don't care.*
>
> *P: You'll care when I take your Nintendo away.*
>
> *C: Here. I don't care.*

This isn't getting very far. The child is so intent on not losing this interactional battle that she has convinced herself that there is nothing wrong and that the parent is just a "raving, mean lunatic." And the parent is actually becoming a raving, mean lunatic in this interaction. The issues of responsibility and helpfulness have been completely lost in the battle for power.

A Strategic Interaction

> *Parent: I noticed a bunch of dishes in your room again.*
>
> *Child: Yeah, I know. I forgot to bring them into the kitchen.*
>
> *P: They sure are hard to clean up when they get that dried out.*
>
> *C: Yeah, I know.*
>
> *P: And I have to admit that all that rotting food in there is a bit gross.*
>
> *C: Yeah, I know.*

Figure 17. *"Irresponsible behavior" is, more than anything, a "hook" for many parents to initiate a power struggle.*

P: Asking you to bring your dishes into the kitchen hasn't seemed to be all that productive.

C: Yeah, I know.

P: Got any suggestions about what we can do about it?

C: I'll just bring my stuff in from now on.

P: Well, you've said that before.

C: Yeah, I know, but I will this time.

P: Great. And, if you don't, I guess I'll have to ground you for an evening, so let me know if you need any help with remembering.

C: OK.

Again, there are no direct accusations, so there is less need for defensiveness. The parent let his desires be known without alienating the child, and even laid down a consequence without creating a battle. Instead of blaming the parent, the child will have to look a little closer at her own responsibility in this matter, especially if she does not want the consequence enforced.

Things to Think About When Your Child Is Irresponsible

❏ Getting angry and yelling may fix the problem—but only temporarily.

❏ Yelling means all the energy is coming from you.

❏ Calm expression of your feeling and a reminder of the consequence help shift the energy to the child. Now *she* has to change to avoid the consequence.

An intent to [teach] can get in the way of [learning]. By doing less, more is accomplished.

—Thomas Moore,
Care of the Soul (1994)

Chapter 10

What Do I Do When...

... My Child Won't Learn from Experience?

If only our children would learn something from all the lessons we try to teach them, we wouldn't have to worry about them when they are grown. We could feel we had done a good job as parents and could now relax. Is that what being grown up is all about—being able to learn from experience? If so, how come so many grown-ups still don't seem to learn from experience? Even adults seem to get into bad situations over and over again. They always seem to be doing things that they should have known better than to do. Why should children be any different?

But then again, when something doesn't work out for some-one— anyone —why in the world would that person do it again?

The Interactional Dynamics

Not learning from experience is part of the irrationality that occurs in a negative interaction. The child is in a position such that "learning the lesson" means losing an interactional battle, losing "face," and losing power. The parent participates in this by using the "lesson" to show the child how she is wrong and how the child "should have listened to me in the first place!"

> *Child (crying): Alicia and the rest of them are so mean! They made fun of me in front of a big group of boys just so they could get a laugh out of the boys. They'll do anything to be popular, and they use me to do it.*

> *Parent: How many times has that happened in the past?*

> *C: Lots of times. It happens all the time.*

> *P: Then why do you hang around with those people? If they were really your friends, they wouldn't hurt you like that.*

> *C (crying harder): They're the only friends I've got. You want me to be all alone?*

> *P: Maybe it would be better to be alone than to be with friends like that! They're always hurting you.*

> *C: They say I'm too sensitive. Maybe that's it. And they're OK if they're not trying to impress someone. I'll just have to get a tougher skin. Maybe I should learn to dish it out like they do.*

> *P: I wouldn't want you to become like one of them. You just said you don't like them for the way they act, and now you're saying you want to be like them. Just get rid of them. You're a nice girl, and there are lots of people who would want to be your friend.*

> *C: Only the nerds and dweebs!*

> *P: Don't talk like that about people. I'm sure they're all very nice people.*

> *C (sarcastically): OK, sure, Mother. Anything you say. I'm going to call Alicia and see what she's doing.*

I'm sure the mother in this example is confused. For once she agreed with her daughter, and she still ended up in an argument with her. She must feel she can't win no matter what she does. Her mistake was trying too soon to help and not finding out what kind of help her daughter wanted. She suggested a solution the daughter could not agree with, then kept trying to make her point so the daughter could learn from this experience. By pushing in a direction the daughter was not ready to go, the mother caused a "reflex" action and the girl went back to where she had been. Anything in the lesson was lost.

A Strategic Interaction

Child (crying): Alicia and the rest of them are so mean! They made fun of me just to impress a bunch of boys.

Parent (sympathetically): Oh, no.

C: Yeah. They're always doing that.

P: It does seem to happen a lot.

C: It happens all the time!

P: That must make you feel pretty rotten.

C: I hate them when they do that.

P: I'll bet you do. (Wondering) Is there anything you can do?

C: I shouldn't hang around with them anymore. It always ends up bad.

P: Well, maybe.

C: Yeah, I'll have to think of something.

P: Let me know how you do with it.

The parent here let the girl talk without trying to fix it for her. She showed support, sympathy, and understanding. She did not fall into the trap of "downing" the friends, which may have caused the girl to defend them.

By taking this rather neutral, curious position, the mother allowed the girl to think about her situation. If the girl is able to think about her situation, she is much more likely to make a good decision about it. She may still be with these friends, but each time they hurt her, she will be able to put that experience and information into her data bank.

Figure 18. *Be careful that when you point out how your child is wrong, you don't increase defensiveness and irrationality.*

Things to Think About When Your Child Won't Learn from Experience

❏ Not learning from experience is part of the irrationality that stems from negative interactions.

❏ As a parent, you should watch that you don't increase defensiveness and irrationality when you point out the child's mistakes.

❏ Find out what kind of help (if any) the child wants before you try to fix the situation.

❏ If the child concludes that you are mean (i.e., a power issue) or don't understand (i.e., an expression issue) when a mistake is pointed out, you should look carefully at your own role in the conversation about the mistake.

Children are entitled to their 'otherness,' as anyone is.

—Alastair Reid,
Places, Poems, Preoccupations (1963)

You gain more influence with your ears than with your mouth.

—Anonymous

Chapter 11

What Do I Do When. . .

. . . My Child "Acts Out" With Drugs, Alcohol, or Sex?

"Acting out" with chemicals or sex can be extremely detrimental to a child's future. Ask anyone who has had to put a child in a chemical abuse treatment center or has had to deal with a pregnant teenager.

The Interactional Dynamics

Many teens "experiment" with drugs and sex. It is part of "experimenting" with life and gaining life experience. Experimenting may not always be harmful in the long run, but there is a fine line between experimenting, overuse, acting out, dependence, and addiction. How can parents know how involved their child is and when they should worry and/or take action?

There is no way to make this judgment if the parents have no open lines of communication with their children. The most important thing, then, is to be able to talk with your child about these things and have your child be able to talk to you. In trying to keep a child from acting out, the wrong interactional moves could push the child further into acting out.

> *Parent: Come here! Where have you been? Your eyes look funny. What are you on? You're on drugs, aren't you?*
>
> *Child: I'm just tired. Leave me alone!*
>
> *P: Drugs and alcohol are bad. You're going to end up just like your Uncle Jimmy.*
>
> *C: Oh, leave me alone. I'm too smart for that. He was an addict. I'll never end up like him.*
>
> *P: Using any kind of drug can lead to addiction. You have to stop now.*
>
> *C: I know lots of kids who use drugs all the time, and they're not having any problems. Just get out of my face.*
>
> *P: I'm taking you right now for a drug screen.*
>
> *C: Oh, come on! I had one beer. Big deal! You try to take me for a drug screen and I'll run away and you'll never see me again.*

If a child looks like he is high and acts like he is high, the chances are that he *is* high on something. If this happens often, the chances are that the child is pretty well involved in substance abuse. The child in this case was immediately defensive about his state and quickly minimized his usage and its effects on him, now and in the future. The parent tried to get him to see that chemicals are bad and that he should reconsider his usage of them. The result, though, was the child's justifying, minimizing, and resorting to irrationality. As with other examples, a parent does not want to alienate the child or put him in an interactional position in which he simply turns off all incoming information from the parent and turns up the volume of his own irrationality.

Whether it is about chemicals or sex, trying to get the child to see the "truth" often puts the child in the position of saying, "It won't happen to me." The more he is made to defend this position, the more he will believe it and the more invincible he will believe he is. Thus, the more vulnerable he becomes.

Figure 19. *Trying to get your child to see the "truth" often puts him in the position of saying, "It won't happen to me."*

A Strategic Interaction

Parent (not unfriendly): Hey! How're you doing? You're late. I was starting to worry about you.

Child: I'm OK. No problem.

P: Wow. Your eyes look funny. (Pause)

C: Yeah, well, I guess I'm tired.

P: *Uh oh. You smell like you've been drinking. (Pause)*

C: *Well, I guess I might have had a beer or two.*

P: *Boy, that really worries me.*

C: *Oh, don't worry. There's nothing wrong with a couple of beers.*

P: *Well, I guess I think about Uncle Jimmy.*

C: *Yeah, well, he was an addict.*

P: *I know. It seems to run in the family. There have been several people who have had problems with drugs and alcohol in the family.*

C: *It won't happen to me.*

P: *I'm glad you can be so sure. I'll still worry, though.*

C: *You worry too much.*

P: *Hey, someone's got to. Can we talk about this some more at another time?*

C: *Sure, but don't worry.*

P: *When we talk, maybe you can give me something not to worry about.*

C: *OK, I will.*

P: *Sounds interesting. I can't wait.*

The parent has shown concern over the situation, has shown that she is aware of the situation, and has indicated that she will keep tabs on the progress of this situation. She has done it, however, from a position of concern, not control. She has not closed off the child to further conversation. In fact, she has opened a forum for discussion of the topic.

She will continue the position of caring concern so that, through upcoming conversations, she will be able to make her points as well as listen to the child. She has faith that, in a good interaction, the child's good sense will be able to come through. The child will be able to use this good sense to make informed decisions rather than act totally out of rebelliousness and irrationality.

The problem is not immediately solved, but the stage is set for the child to solve his own problem or avoid a problem in the first place.

Things to Think About When Your Child Acts Out

❏ Keep lines of communication open by listening.

❏ The more the child is put into a position of defending himself (i.e., "it won't happen to me"), the more dangerous the situation and the more vulnerable he is.

❏ Be concerned about what you see and suspect. You don't have to have irrefutable proof. Suspicion of drug involvement can be enough to justify some form of consequence (for example, drug testing).

❏ If you have to get irrefutable proof, then you are expending all the energy. If the child has to act in such a way as to keep your suspicion down, then he is expending the energy. Let him be in the position of trying to convince you that he isn't doing anything rather than your trying to prove that he is.

Your mother and I are just trying
to understand, Nathan, what sort
of statement you feel you would
be making with a pierced
nipple.

Chapter 12

What Do I Do When. . .

. . . My Child Shows Poor Judgment and Is Easily Influenced?

I see many kids in my psychotherapy practice. They get into all kinds of trouble. After learning why the child is being brought to me and after hearing from the parents all the things they are worried about regarding this kid, I start to worry about how bad off he seems. How could anyone get into that kind of situation if he had any sense at all?

Then I meet and talk with the child. I usually find a rather pleasant person who has quite a bit of insight into his situation and who seems very rational. I wonder how this child could make the kind of decisions that would lead him into the trouble he is in. It doesn't make sense.

The Interactional Dynamics

There is more good sense in our children than we often get to see. When we are not seeing that sense, it means that we are in some sort of negative interaction where the *irrational* reigns. Then, of course, when we try to point out how irrational our child is being, we put him into the position of believing and defending his position.

Child: I'm going to kill those guys!

Parent: You will do no such thing! Don't talk such nonsense!

C: You watch me. They're not going to bother me again.

P: Stop that crazy talk, and tell me what happened.

C: It's not crazy. They're threatening to beat me up if I don't give them money, and I'm not going to take it. I'm going to get a gun. Then watch what happens if they mess with me.

P: Oh, right! Then you're going to jail and you'll get kicked out of school and lose all your privileges.

C: Big deal! I don't care. Nobody's going to push me around anymore.

P: Besides, where are you going to get a gun?

C: I can get one easy. I know lots of people who have them. I'll steal one if I have to.

P: If you don't stop that talk right now, you'll be punished.

C: I don't care. You're not going to push me around either.

This child is so upset that he is not thinking about the consequences of his actions. The *immediate* is what is important. That's how people make poor decisions and get into trouble. They only think of "now." In this interaction, the parent's attempts to calm the child and get him to think of what he is saying only seem to get the child talking more and more about his irrational plan.

The anger and irrationality even get transferred to the parent when the child begins to threaten the parent. The parent has inadvertently challenged the child to find a way to carry out the plan. Also, if the child backs down from the plan now, he will be doing what "Mommy/Daddy" wants. That makes it even more important to carry out this terrible plan.

A Strategic Interaction

Child: I'm going to kill those guys!

Parent: Wow! You are really angry. What happened?

C: These kids threatened to beat me up if I don't give them money. I'm going to get a gun. Then watch what happens when they mess with me.

P: Yeah. That's scary. No wonder you want to kill them.

C: Nobody's messing with me!

P: I hope not. [Pause] Is there anything you can do other than shooting them to keep them from messing with you?

C: I don't know.

P: Well, I'd sure hate to see you get in trouble by taking a gun to school, much less the trouble you'd get into if you used the gun.

C: Yeah, but I'm not going to get beat up.

P: I don't blame you. What can we do instead? I'll help any way I can.

C: Maybe you can talk to the principal or the parents or the police or something.

P: Good idea. I'll talk to the principal to see if she is aware of the problem and if she has any suggestions about fixing it. If not, and we have to go to the police, we will. I'll make the call first thing in the morning.

The parent was able to listen to the child's anger without becoming so alarmed that he cut off communication. When the child was convinced that the parent saw the situation the way he saw it, the child was ready to hear alternatives rather than escalating into more anger and violence.

Things to Think About When Your Child Shows Poor Judgment

❑ Your children have more good sense than you think.

❑ Poor decisions are often the result of negative interactions that increase irrationality.

❑ Don't inadvertently challenge or encourage your child to act out the irrationality.

❑ Listen. Ask how you can help.

❑ Stay connected for the possibility of *future* interactions.

There is nothing wrong with teenagers that reasoning with won't aggravate.

—Unknown

Chapter 13

What Do I Do When...

... My Child Won't Listen to Reason?

When a child is not being reasonable or is coming up with ridiculous statements, she may or may not know she is being ridiculous. The statements may come from a lack of correct information, or she may be trying to get a "rise" out of her parents. Either way she is a challenge to a parent. The tendency is to "set her straight." Whether or not the child believes what she is saying, "setting her straight" is a guaranteed way of "setting her in cement." The child gets caught up in the negative interaction, defending her position and convincing herself more and more that there is logic in her ridiculousness.

The Interactional Dynamics

An example comes from a residential program for teens in trouble. In an informal discussion about what the girls in the program wanted to do when they got older, one girl said that she wanted to be a madam and run a brothel. Of course, the program was supposed to teach girls to be proud, respect themselves, and shoot for the very best they could be. Running a whorehouse was not a vocation the counselors thought was particularly appropriate. They saw this as a failure on their part and decided that it needed correction. They called for a group discussion, which happened any time there was a problem in the group. The discussion time was used for the group as a whole to evaluate and handle the problem. In this case, the group was to explore with this girl her decision to be a madam and to talk her out of it.

The group spent hours with the girl, showing her in every way possible why she should strive for something else. The girl found more and more reasons why being a madam was the most wonderful profession in the world. Not only the counselors, but all of the other girls in the program, spent a lot of time and energy trying to get this girl to listen to reason. They only seemed to be convincing her more to pursue her supposedly chosen profession.

A Strategic Interaction

A supervising counselor had seen the group assemble and had overheard parts of the discussion. At the time, she had no training in Strategic Interaction, yet her intervention was quite effective.

Supervisor: What is it you want to be?

Child: I want to be a madam.

S: Oh. Well, I hope you're the best one you can be.

C: Yeah, thanks.

The group discussion ended. Nothing was ever heard again of her wanting to be a madam. The power struggle ended.

As soon as you assume the position of taking the child seriously and respond with a sincere "Oh. Really?" the child cannot fight against you by defending her position. When she doesn't have to defend her position, she has to look at it more realistically. She is suddenly fully enmeshed in the silliness of her statements and thought processes. You can actually see the dawning embarrassment in her face. She may not show you right away that she has begun to consider alternatives, but it is probably happening.

Figure 20. *If all the energy for realistically examining the situation comes from the parent, the child will never have to do it herself.*

Things to Think About When Your Child Won't Listen to Reason

❑ Taking a *listening, interested* position ends the power struggle, especially if the struggle was because the child wouldn't listen to "reasonable arguments."

❑ When the child doesn't have to defend her position, she can look at it more realistically.

❏ If all the energy comes from the parent to examine the situation realistically, the child will never have to do it herself.

❏ "Reason" is often power cloaked in adult language.

"He does not have a discipline problem! He's just had a little too much sugar, that's all."

Chapter 14

with Allison Sallee, M.A.

What Do I Do When. . .

. . . My Child Is Violent?

Teens and their families can get into very intense, serious interactions. This can also happen with younger children, though. The dynamics and solutions are similar. The following example involves a nine-year-old boy and his family.

The parents had divorced and, as is common, friction between Mom and Father remained. The boy, we'll call him John, had a brother, Billy, six years old. Both stayed with Mom and visited Father on weekends. John had always been somewhat of a behavior problem, mostly at home, but his behavior had become considerably worse since the divorce.

Mom had tried many things to gain control of John. She tried grounding, removal of privileges (no TV, no outside play, no dessert), spanking, and physical restraint methods. Mom often had to call Father to come over and settle John down. Still, no matter what she did, the incidents degenerated into screaming matches and physical power struggles. She worked hard at keeping a positive, loving, and accepting attitude toward John. It seems that the things she tried, many of which could have been recommended by therapists and parenting experts, should have worked but didn't.

One evening Mom tried to get John to put on more appropriate pants before going out to dinner, but he refused. He became verbally abusive and began to threaten physical assault on Mom. At one point she had to restrain him physically but eventually left him in the room to change his clothes. Instead, though, he pulled a clock off the wall and kicked a hole in the wall.

This incident helped convince her to bring the boy to therapy. He was also escalating his negative behavior at school. He was beginning to refuse to do what teachers asked of him. One time he began screaming when he didn't want to do something. The principal was also becoming concerned about his behavior.

Surely, Mom thought, the boy was exhibiting problems from the divorce. Also, Mom knew that Father had a drinking problem and did not spend much time with the kids when they were at his home. She was, then, also very invested in getting the father to therapy. Father went one or two times, usually arriving very late. John did not like going to therapy, and getting him there was always a struggle for Mom.

John's problems continued to escalate.

Once, John wanted to be the one to start the video the family had rented, but his brother beat him to it. John got very angry and began verbally abusing Mom (telling her how much he hated her and hated living there). He was obviously escalating toward violent behavior.

Mom took Billy and left the room to give John a chance to calm down. Instead, he went on a rampage. He pulled pictures off the wall, broke the frames and glass, and threw a candlestick through a front window.

Another time Mom was making coke floats as a treat for the boys. John wanted more ice cream for his, but Mom thought he had had enough. They argued, then John tried to get to the freezer to get more. Mom blocked the freezer and struggled with John to get him to give up his quest for the ice cream. Finally he claimed that he "didn't want it anyway." She turned away momentarily and, when she turned back, he smiled at her while he poured his drink over the business paperwork she had been working on at the table, ruining it all.

Yet another time they argued about cleaning up a sidewalk where they had drawn a hop-scotch area. Mom gave simple instructions and turned to go. He threw a broom at her, bruising her legs.

Indeed, Mom came every week with bruises on her arms and legs from altercations she had with John.

This was a serious situation. Mom felt very angry, frustrated, scared, and out of control. At just nine years old, John was totally "out of control" (or totally *in control of the interactions*). Mom was afraid of him and was being hurt by him almost every day. At this age, she could still win a physical battle, but it would not be long before that changed. Billy, the six-year-old, was also frightened and angry and complained often about his brother's behavior.

In general, even when there weren't physical altercations, John was not pleasant to be with. He complained constantly when things didn't go his way and, with his history of physical attacks, Mom was always on edge.

The situation became so unmanageable that Mom had to let John stay at his father's house. Billy felt left out from his father's attentions with this arrangement and also went to Father's. Interestingly, most of the abusive instances happened when John was with his mother for visitation, so the move to his father's did not solve things.

The Interactional Dynamics

In situations where violence occurs or is threatened, the negative interaction has gone far beyond the usual limits. Power and expression issues have remained unsatisfactorily resolved for some time. As the situation gets more tense and violence seems more likely, the parent, usually out of fear, tries harder to control the child with more power. This leads the child to have to use more power in return, and the situation quickly deteriorates. In effect the parent is saying, "I will make you act right!" The child responds, "I will continue to act this way and, to prove it, I will act worse. You can't control me!"

It would be easy in this case to blame the divorce, the less-than-perfect father, the mother, or a diagnosis of the boy (Attention Deficit Disorder, Oppositional Defiant Disorder, Depression, or some chemical imbalance, for example) for these problems. The mother, though, is an intelligent, knowledgeable woman who genuinely cares about her children. She knows child development and proper discipline techniques. She really has tried many things that should have worked. So why didn't they work?

Looking at the problem as residing within any of the particular participants misses the interactional aspects. This is a case with many tangled, sometimes subtle, power struggles. The physical interactions were obvious power struggles. Less obvious were Mom's struggles in trying to change the child and in trying to change the father (by getting him to stop drinking and by getting him to come to therapy). The physical altercations were signs of the generally ineffective power struggles that were occurring. The overall interactions had to change.

A Strategic Interaction

The first thing Mom had to do was "give up"; that is, she had to stop trying to change things. This would be like taking a weak position, in which she would be admitting that she really could not make the boy or his father be different. She did this in different ways:

- She quit trying to get John to come to therapy.
- She quit trying to get the father to come to therapy.

- She stopped trying to restrain John physically.

- If she had to get Father to come and intervene, she stopped protecting John from the father's punishment.

- She stopped nagging, screaming, and arguing.

- She quit looking for "why?" Instead of looking for a diagnosis or a psychological/emotional problem, she concentrated on the interactions, no matter what the cause.

- She ended the power struggles. In many small ways she replaced power struggles with alternative positions.

For example, John was supposed to take medication for his diagnosed ADHD. Getting him to take it had been a struggle every morning. She changed that by simply putting the pill and water in front of him and saying, "Here's your medication." If he said anything about it, she just ignored it. Remarkably, he took his medication and they avoided any struggle about it.

During national scholastic testing, Mom wanted John not only to eat a good breakfast, but also to have a mid-morning snack so he would be able to think and perform well. Mom conveniently worked at the same school John attended, so she frequently had snacks available for him. However, the conversations usually went like this:

Mother: Here's a snack. You'll need it.

Child: No! I don't want it.

M: You'll need nourishment. Eat!

C: No! I don't want it!

This went on until both Mom and John were angry and frustrated, but John never ate the snack.

She changed that to the following:

M: I have a snack here if you want it. You know where it is.

In this interaction, there was no battle, no frustration, no bad feelings. Sometimes John came and got a snack; sometimes he didn't. He got a snack when he was hungry and didn't when he was not, which is as it should be.

Mom liked to do family activities with the children. The kids often wanted to go Rollerblading. However, as soon as they would start out, John would start complaining about something – the road was too rough, it was too hot, he didn't want to go that way. Mom usually responded like this:

> *M: Well, you're the one who wanted to go Rollerblading. It's not so bad. Come on; have a better attitude!*

The result of this was more complaining by John, an escalation of anger, and fear on Mom's part that there would be another out-of-control incident. She changed those interactions to the following:

> *M: Yes, it is rather [hot, rough, bad]. Would you rather quit?*

John would then grudgingly state his desire to continue and would stop complaining. Here, Mom acknowledged the complaint but did not get hooked into arguing, comforting, or trying to fix the problem, so the issue passed quickly.

For the big things, when John became verbally abusive, heading toward being physically abusive, Mom had to do something very different from what she had been doing. Previously, she would scold, warn of punishment, and restrain as the situation escalated. Now she handled it differently:

> *M (as calmly as possible): If this continues, we'll have to stop.*

Or,

> *M: You won't be able to come next week if you do that.*

Of course, at first he did it anyway. If they were involved in an activity and he reacted badly, she would immediately end her own participation in it. If he did throw a tantrum, the next week she would call him and calmly remind him that he would not be able to come over until Saturday, instead of Friday. Since he seemed so angry with her, one would think that he would not care if he saw her or not. Often he responded with:

C: I don't care. I don't want to see you anyway.

She would then answer,

M: Okay. I just wanted to remind you.

Then she would end the call. Amazingly, though, he would come on Saturday and be better behaved and more pleasant.

By keeping the Business side consistent, while she maintained the Personal side, she was able to make a difference. After four to six weeks of paying close attention to the interactions, staying out of all the little power struggles that John offered her, and calmly enforcing consequences (ending the activity or not allowing the activity or visitation the next time), the violent incidents stopped. Mom felt she could quit her consultations with us because the situation had improved, she felt more in control, and she was enjoying her children again.

At the last session, Mom told of an incident that illustrated the changes. She and the boys had been playing basketball when John became upset over something and began to misbehave. Mom told him he would have to have a five-minute time-out because of his behavior and asked him to go back to the apartment to serve it. The apartment living room window overlooked the basketball court. Instead of arguing and fighting, John went to the apartment. A few months before this, Mom would have expected John to do something drastic and destructive in the apartment. This time, however, when she looked up at the apartment window, she saw John calmly watching Mom and his brother play. After five minutes, he returned to the game and played appropriately.

In cases that involve violence, we sometimes make the mistake of paying attention only to the violent interactions when the whole series of interactions needs to be changed. Getting out of all the small ways the mother was in a power struggle was just as important in this case as intervening in the violent episodes.

Consider another example of violence. A 15-year-old boy lived with his father, who had been separated from the boy's mother for about a year. A younger daughter lived with the mother. Mother and Father were reconciling, and Mother was moving back in the home. The problem was that the boy was very angry at the mother and the "bratty" sister. He thought his father was "stupid" for reconciling, and he made it clear that he was against this move. In fact, he made veiled and vague threats that "if she crosses me, then it's her fault if something happens to her." The mother was frightened by this threat. When Father tried to talk him out of his feelings and get him to accept the situation, the boy seemed more determined to disrupt, by physical means if necessary, this happy homecoming.

I suggested that the father talk to the boy and, without threatening, calmly tell him something like this:

> F: *Look, I just want you to know that if there is ever any violence, if anyone ever gets hurt or is even threatened, I will have to call the police. That won't be tolerated.*

The boy was quiet and thoughtful for a moment and asked,

> Son: *Dad? You'd really call the police on me?*

> F: *I'd have to. Believe me, I'd never want to do that, but I won't have violence in my home.*

Rather than talking about what he would do to punish and control the child, the father was able to communicate a regretful, sad warning about steps he would have to take if the situation arose. The difference is subtle, but important. The Business side is clear, but the Personal side is also. It was important that the father add that he would never want to do it, and that he say it in such a way that the boy believed him.

Things to Think About When Your Child Is Violent

❏ Parents have to give the message that violence is not acceptable under any circumstance. They will not engage in it, nor will they will tolerate it from their children.

❏ Whenever the parents act violently, children get the message that it is OK to act violently, no matter what the parents *say* about it.

❏ In extreme cases, police or other authorities may have to be called, not only to protect the family but also to give the strong message that violence is not acceptable. The parent's position, though, is not "See! I gotcha!" Rather, it would be, "I'm terribly sorry that it had to come to that. I hated doing that to you, and I don't ever want to have to do it again. I will, though, if we can't find another way to settle our differences. Do you have any suggestions?"

❏ Violence may be a large part of some children's culture, and they may be in the habit of solving problems that way. Parents may have to offer alternatives. For example:

> *Parent: It seems you are very angry right now. How about if we both take a few minutes to cool down and continue this later?*
>
> or
>
> *P: We're both mad right now. I think I'll take a walk and think about what we've said so far. I'll calm down and we'll discuss it more later.*
>
> or
>
> *P: I can see you are really angry. It's not OK to take it out on me, but why don't you go beat your mattress?*

❏ Power begets the need for power, and violence begets the need for violence.

❏ The whole set of interactions needs to be examined and changed. It is a mistake to focus only on the violent interactions.

The ultimate hollow victory is to win a game no one else is playing.

—Jamie Raser,
Parenting the Difficult Child Workshop
(1993)

Chapter 15

What Do I Do When. . .

. . . My Child Won't Obey Rules?

Arguments between adolescents and families about "rules" seem to be universal. The teen feels old enough to make his own decisions about curfew, chores, school, and other subjects. Parents often try to explain that the child is still young and immature and does not really know yet what is best for him. That being the case, the parents still make the rules.

A father consulted with me about his 17-year-old son who was very difficult to manage. The most recent incident involved a weekend when the father was out of town on business. He made it clear that the son was to have no guests over to the house when the father was gone. The father was concerned about what would happen when he was not there to supervise and chaperone.

When he returned home, the father found obvious signs that many people had been to his home. Although there was no physical damage to the house, missing were two steaks, a pound of hamburger, a package of hot dogs, two loaves of bread, two boxes of crackers, a six-pack of beer, and two six-packs of sodas. There were also trash bags stacked in the garage (maybe he should have been thankful for that) and evidence of cigarette smoking.

The father was angry and concerned about the obvious flaunting of the rule of "no guests." He thought he had to gain control over the boy and could not let him get away with this show of disrespect. He called me to get my opinion of his solution. His thought was to change the locks on the doors and not give his son a key. This, he thought, would teach the boy the consequences of his action.

The Interactional Dynamics

You may see rules as a way to help your child, your family, and/or yourself. Your teenager probably sees rules as a power play on your part. Anyone who sets rules must be powerful, and the rules are a testament to that power. Also, although the rules are meant to help you navigate your world, they interfere in the world of the teenager.

Rules can imply that you don't see the child as a grown-up, as a responsible person, or as someone who can be trusted. This may actually be the way you see your child. For the child to accept the rules, then, is to accept an unattractive and demeaning picture of himself. To accept rules is also an immediate loss of power. A rule tends to be what one person demands and forces on another person. It is usually not a collaborative effort, meaning that it is passed from "on high" down to the recipients who have no voice and no choice in the matter.

Viewed in this way, it is not surprising that an adolescent may feel that he has to fight against rules.

A Strategic Interaction

I told the father in this example that since I thought this was a serious situation, it was very important to handle it well. This son and father had a long history of conflict, and the boy was getting more and more belligerent. The power struggle was escalating. I saw changing the locks as more escalation of that struggle. In that case, the boy would not learn anything from that consequence. He would only see his father as being mean, unfair, and rejecting. This would justify, in his mind, finding ways around the consequence. I predicted that he would find ways to break into the house if he were locked out. The father admitted that the boy threatened to do this when the lock-out was mentioned. I also predicted that the boy would be able to blame his father for any action he did since his father "unfairly" locked him out. "If he hadn't locked me out, I wouldn't have had to break that window to get in!"

To do something different, then, and to get out of the power struggle, I suggested he have a conversation with his son that might go like this:

> *Father: I'm disappointed that you had people over. It is not okay with me for you to do that. It makes it very hard to trust you. If it happens again, I'll have to think of something more drastic to handle the situation.*

Here the father was able to state how he felt about the situation without being angry, which would only have alerted his son's self-defense system. Since the irrationality was not escalated by anger, the boy was much more likely to pay attention to the possible consequences of his actions. If the lock-out measure had been implemented at that time, the boy could easily think, "Well, I'm already locked out of my own house. What else can happen to me?" and use that reasoning to justify any misbehavior.

Because the father is being fair and rational and has not escalated irrationality in the boy, the boy may be able to think better next time and make a better decision. If the next time the boy still did not make a better decision, the father is in a very good position to impose a consequence without it seeming like "meanness" on his part. It will be much easier to see the consequence as a result of the boy's actions, after fair and rational warning.

Things to Think About When Your Child Won't Obey Rules

❏ In severe battles over rules, changing the interaction is the primary goal in the beginning. As interactions around the rules and around the breaking of those rules improves, the child will come around to being more cooperative.

❏ Rules come under the Business side of the relationship, but it is important to keep the Personal side involved also, ensuring that respect, trust, and, hopefully, collaboration are included and emphasized.

❏ Rules become easier to enforce when they don't carry as many power issues. In fact, as interactions improve and the child's rationality increases, the need for rules diminishes.

❏ Using the phrase, "Come to me with an alternate plan," is a good one in situations where you feel comfortable with some negotiation around rules. It shows a willingness to collaborate, which shows respect for the child. That goes a long way in turning off the irrationality in the child.

Children should be led into the right paths,
not by severity, but by persuasion.

—Terence,
The Brothers (160 BC)

Chapter 16

What Do I Do When. . .

. . . My Child Is In a Gang, Hangs with a Bad Crowd, Or Is Prone to Peer Pressure?

Gangs are everywhere. They're getting more numerous, and they're getting more active. Gangs range from the very organized, criminal groups that started in California and are spreading around the United States to loosely organized groups of "wannabe" kids. The existence of a gang in a school creates the need for other kids to organize themselves into their own group just to protect themselves from the original gang. Thus, gangs and undesirable groups proliferate.

Most gangs involve violence and illegal activities. When in a gang, there is always the threat of violence from a rival gang or trouble from police because of illegal activities. Why would anyone want to live a life of constant threat and danger?

The Interactional Dynamics

As hard as it might be to believe, gangs offer some children everything they never got, or never thought they got, at home. Gangs have clear rules and guidelines. A child knows exactly what is expected of her. When the rules are followed, the child gets rewarded, praised, and accepted. The rules and guidelines fit more closely with the teen culture than do those of the adult's society, so they are easier for the child to follow.

A gang provides a way for the child to gain status and importance. That is often not possible in a family. In a family, a child will always be a child and is often treated like one even beyond the time she leaves the family. The gang immediately treats the child like she is important and offers ways for her to be even more important. These ways often involve rebellious, anti-authority actions, but that fits right into what the child is doing anyway as part of growing up and gaining a separate identity. The gang culture exploits this developmental need.

Parents could actually learn from gang culture. Gangs must be doing something right if they can attract such loyalty, even though the children are at risk of losing their lives or their freedom when with the gang. A child may want to leave a family because she is asked to take out the garbage while a gang gets even more loyalty for asking the child to rob a store or participate in a gang fight.

Why don't children see what they are getting into? There is real attraction to elements of the gang culture, but there are also many bad things about gangs that children do not seem to realize.

Not realizing the danger of a gang is part of the irrationality that happens in a negative interaction. The stronger the need for a separate identity, freedom, power, status, and positive self-image, the more prone the child will be to ignore the dangers of a gang. When these needs are strong, the *rational* will be ignored. The parent's attempts to explain the dangers will also be ignored. In fact, a negative interaction is set up when a parent attempts to show the child the danger. This only produces more irrational defenses and more loyalty to the gang. As the parent becomes more and more concerned and angry about the child's involvement in the gang, he increases his attack on the gang and inadvertently increases the child's loyalty.

The way to reduce the chances that a child will be attracted to a gang is to deal with the child with positive interactions throughout her life. When the child begins the process of separation and shows the need for identity and positive self-image, it is especially important that the parent react with Strategic Interactions.

If the child has gotten involved in a gang or seems to be heading in that direction and all other attempts at resolving this crisis have failed, Strategic Interaction can improve the relationship between parent and child and arrange it so that the child may be able to look at her involvement more realistically and rationally. The final decision to be in a gang or leave one can only come from the child. Strategic Interactions can help a child make the right choices.

A Strategic Interaction

At one of my parenting seminars, Joe and Mary Smith (not their real names) asked for help with the following situation. They had been having trouble with their 13-year-old daughter, Sue (not her real name). She had gotten involved with a gang. In fact, she had become the girlfriend of the gang leader. She had been staying away from the house for several nights at a time and had become involved with the juvenile authorities. Interactions with her parents had come to the point where both she and the parents were losing control of themselves.

It had gotten so bad that the Smiths placed Sue in a residential treatment center. As was the policy of the center, Sue came home four days a month. When she came home, though, she continued seeing the gang leader and staying out all weekend. The struggles to keep her from going out also continued. The Smiths pleaded, yelled, held her, locked her in her room, nailed the windows shut, and did everything else they could think of. After hours of turmoil, Sue usually succeeded in getting out anyway. Often, the situation became violent, with either Sue or her parents threatening injury. A complicating factor was that the gang began to threaten the family, saying that they would do harm to the family if Sue was not allowed to come out. The Smiths ended this description by saying, "And she's coming home tomorrow for another weekend visit. What should we do?"

Before I gave advice, I made sure they had done everything in their power, including calling the police for help, and that nothing had worked. I asked if they were ready to try something else. The direction of my intervention was away from trying to control her and toward staying out of the power struggle that they always seemed to lose. I asked them to make a simple statement to Sue:

> P: *It is not OK with us for you to go out. We feel it is very dangerous out there and we worry about you a lot.*

Period! Nothing more. If she argued, explained, or continued with, "Well, I don't care what you think. I'm going anyway!" they were simply to repeat, "It's not OK with us. We worry."

Staying out of the power struggle was the most important thing for them to do at this point. The Smiths agreed that they would stay out of a violent confrontation with Sue in this way, but, of course, they were still very frightened about the situation. I explained that, by taking this position with her, they were actually more likely to get cooperative behavior from her eventually.

The parents bravely did as I instructed and Sue did go out with her gang friends that Friday night and did stay out all night. However, she called late in the evening to say that she was all right. That was a change! She came home the next morning, and the Smiths reported that she was more pleasant than usual for the rest of the weekend. Then, on Monday, when Sue got off the bus back at the treatment center, she suddenly broke into tears and fell into the arms of her counselor. Asked what was wrong, she replied that she did not like the way her boyfriend and his friends treated her family. This, of course, was also different and the first time she showed any concern for the safety of her family or even awareness that their safety was threatened. Several months later, Sue had broken up with her boyfriend and the relationship with her parents was much improved.

The Smiths and Sue were in such a power struggle that nothing was being accomplished. Anything the Smiths were trying to teach Sue about the dangers of her friendships and her actions were lost in Sue's increased irrationality. The Smiths' irrationality was shown by their continuing to struggle with Sue when it was very apparent that the situation was only getting worse. In this power struggle, Sue was easily able to avoid responsibility for her behavior and blame her parents for anything that went wrong, however irrational that was. As soon as the Smiths took a different position with her, avoided the power struggle, and used a Strategic Interaction, Sue's irrationality lowered enough for her to see the situation as it really was and also to take responsibility for it.

This, of course, does not mean that there will never be problems between them again. Life and relationships are difficult. However, the more that parents use Strategic Interactions, the more they will be building responsibility, maturity, decision-making skills, and the kind of positive relationship that will see them through the hard times when they come.

Things to Think about When Your Child Is in A Gang

❏ Create ways for your child to be able to gain respect and privilege in your family.

❏ Your attempts to get your child to see the dangers of the gang or peer group may cause irrational defense of the group. It is okay to express your feelings, but do it in a way that doesn't increase defensiveness.

❏ Gangs are hard to get out of once someone is in. The child may not be able to stop all his activity immediately.

❏ Better interactions between parent and child will satisfy the needs that are presently filled by the gang.

❑ Strategic Interactions can reduce the irrationality so that the child can see the situation more realistically and make more appropriate decisions.

In the little world in which children have their existence, there is nothing so finely perceived as injustice.

—Charles Dickens,
Great Expectations (1861)

Chapter 17

What Do I Do When. . .

. . . My Child Seems Depressed?

Change is a large part of adolescents' lives. They have much to think about and much to be concerned about. Sometimes all of this gets them down. That is no different from what happens with adults. Teens, though, have fewer resources to handle difficulties and less experience with hard times. They also, by nature of their developmental stage, are more impulsive and do not think things through very well. They may resort to drastic means when they are worried about something.

Although many teenagers go through hard times and come out very well, some get quite depressed, even resorting to suicide. A child who resorts to suicide has somehow decided that killing himself is a rational alternative, and maybe the only alternative.

The Interactional Dynamics

An adolescent with a problem is in a bind. She wants someone with whom she can talk, who will listen, who will offer good advice, and whom she respects. However, she doesn't want to feel she is being "dependent" or "childish" in getting this advice. Sometimes she may just want to talk it out without getting advice. Talking to a parent about problems interferes with the child's privacy, attempted independence and separation, and budding feelings of self-confidence and competence.

> *Parent: You've been moping around here for weeks now. What in the world is wrong with you?*
>
> *Child: Nothing.*
>
> *P: I know it can't be "nothing." I know you. I know something is wrong. What is it?*
>
> *C: You don't know me! You don't know anything about me.*
>
> *P: Well, maybe that's because you never talk to me!*
>
> *C: You never listen when I do talk. Why should I talk to you?*
>
> *P: I'm your parent. I can help you.*
>
> *C: You don't understand anything, and you can't help with anything. Just leave me alone.*

This parent's concern for the child, his desire to know the problem, and his wish to help turned into an argument about whether there was something wrong, how uncommunicative the child was, whether the parent really could understand, and whether the parent really could help. The attempt to get closer to the child ended up pushing the child farther away. Instead of lines of communication being opened, they became, it seems, more closed.

What was supposed to be a helpful discussion became an argument. If the child was depressed before, she may be more depressed now because it seems that this important person in her life, her parent, is not someone to whom she can talk. That can make the child feel even more alone.

A Strategic Interaction

Parent: You know, it seems that you've been kind of down lately. [Pause]

Child: Yeah?

P: Yeah. That's how it has seemed to me anyway.

C: [No response]

P: I've been kind of worried. Something going on?

C: I'm all right.

P: I sure am available to listen anytime you want to talk.

C: Thanks. I don't think anyone can help with this problem.

P: Wow. It must be a bad one. [Pause] I'm willing to hear it, though, and see if there's anything we might be able to come up with.

C: It's about a boy at school, but I don't really want to talk about it. There's nothing you can do.

P: Maybe not. I'm sure you've tried lots of things already. [Pause] Can you tell me anything about it?

C: Well, [begins to give some details of the problem].

This parent, even though quite concerned, was very careful to give the child "room." Giving room, acknowledging how bad the problem must be, recognizing the child's attempts to solve the problem up to now, and offering only a "listening ear" at this time showed a great deal of respect for the child. The child responded by leaking small bits of information. This would continue to happen if the parent continued this slow, respectful tact.

The parent could also offer to put the child in touch with someone else:

P: You seem to like to talk to [Aunt May, Mr. Smith down the street] sometimes. Have you thought about talking to her/ him about this?

C: No, not really.

P: Well, he would probably be more than willing to listen. If there's anything I can do to help set up a way for you to talk to someone else, I'd be very happy to. Your counselor at school may be someone to talk to, or if you wanted, we could set an appointment with a therapist. Do any of those sound like options for you?

C: I don't know. I'll think about it.

P: Good. Let me know.

Figure 21. *Be careful to allow the child to feel competent, confident, and independent even though she wants help.*

Offering options is important, **but the options are not about solutions at this point.** The parent is still trying to enter the child's world. Once there, the parent may be able to make suggestions that the child will be able to listen to. Throughout this exchange, the parent has not tried to talk the child out of the seriousness of the problem. Instead, the parent has shown respect for the child and the child's evaluation of the situation. The parent has shown that options are available while still maintaining an attitude of respect and noninterference.

If the child does not respond to the above conversation and still appears unusually despondent, more action may be needed.

Parent: I've really become worried about you.

Child: Why?

P: You don't seem to be eating or sleeping, and your school work has suffered. What can we do about this? It's been a long time now.

C: There's nothing to do.

P: Unless you can think of something else, I'm going to make an appointment with a therapist.

C: I'm not going to any shrink!

P: Unless something else happens, I'm going to make the appointment. If you hate the person after three sessions and it isn't helping, we'll try something else. Maybe the therapist can suggest something for me to do to not worry so much. I don't know. I can't go on watching you like this, though. I'm very worried.

The parent offers therapy while still allowing room for the child to come up with an alternative plan or to change the behavior so the parent does not worry so much. A trial of three sessions is also offered to reduce immediate defensiveness.

Often, a child who is really depressed loses so much momentum that she cannot make the first move. When someone takes charge and gets help for the child, even though she may fight against it, she is relieved to get it. The trick of Strategic Interaction is to keep defensiveness down enough so that the child will be able to partake of the help offered without feeling that she is "losing face."

Things to Think About When Your Child Is Depressed

❏ Teens have fewer resources to help them handle difficulties and they have less experience with hard times than adults do.

❏ Listen thoughtfully and respectfully. Determine what help the child wants; she may just want you to listen.

❏ Be careful to allow the child to feel competent, confident, and independent even though she needs or wants help.

❏ Be sure to interact in such a way as to keep lines of communication open. If they seem to be closing instead, back up and try again from a different tack.

❏ Steps to good listening:

    a. Acknowledge the child's upset or concern.

    b. Acknowledge the child's attempts to solve the problem.

    c. Listen.

❏ Offer the assistance of a counselor, therapist, or trusted adult to help.

❏ If the situation does not improve, or if you are worried about suicide or other serious behavior, make an appointment with a therapist and "gently demand" the child try it for three sessions.

Tis skill, not strength, that governs a ship.

—Thomas Fuller, M.D.,
Gnomologia (1732)

Section 3

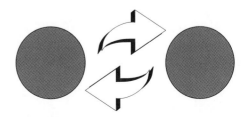

After learning the tricks of the trade, many think they know the trade.

—Anonymous

It is sometimes easier to head an institute for the study of child guidance than it is to turn one brat into a decent human being.

—Joseph Wood Krutch, "Whom Do We Picket Tonight?" in *If You Don't Mind My Saying So* (1964)

Chapter 18

What Do I Do When "Nothing" Seems to Work?

There are times when nothing seems to work. No matter what you do, your child does not respond. There may be several reasons for this:

❑ The negative interactions may have been occurring for so long that they are so much of a habit, they seem impossible to break.

❑ The child may continue to be exposed to negative interactions in environments over which you have no control, such as at the divorced parent's home.

❏ Chemical abuse may be severely reducing the child's capacity to think and behave rationally. No amount of Strategic Interaction can make a person sober.

❏ The habit of negative interaction may have become so ingrained that it is now a personality trait instead of just a poor way of behaving and thinking. Personalities are much more difficult to change than interactions.

❏ There could be a true psychological problem so severe that it affects the child's ability to think and behave appropriately.

❏ A physiological or neurological problem may be present which affects thinking and behaving.

Ask Yourself These Questions

➡ *Am I truly following all of the tenets of the* **Parent's Creed***?*

➡ *Have I given* **Strategic Interaction** *enough time to make a difference?*

If you feel you have done everything as well as you can (consulting a psychotherapist, family therapist, or child/parenting expert; attending parenting groups; getting all the suggestions about Strategic Interactions that you can) and there is still no change, you should consider checking out physiological, neurological, and chemical abuse problems. You may also consider alternative placement for your child. The following is an example of how this might be approached.

A Strategic Interaction When "Nothing" Is Working

Parent (calmly but with feeling): I have to tell you that I am quite disappointed that things aren't working out better between us.

Child (angrily): Big deal! Things are fine, if you'd just keep your trap shut!

P: Yeah, well I've tried to do the best I could. I'm sorry you are still not happy about the way things are going around here. I'm not very happy about it either. It just doesn't seem to be working out. Do you have any ideas about what we can do about it?

C: Sure. Just shut up and leave me alone!

P: I guess I'm doing that as much as I'm able and we're both still unhappy. Maybe we should consider someplace else for you to live.

C: Great! I'll go live with my father.

P: That is an option we can check out. Why don't you call him and see what he says?

C: Or I could live with Jimmy and his mother. They'll take me in.

P: That wouldn't be my favorite option. We can look into it though. There is a question of legal and financial responsibility that we would have to check out. You might see if Jimmy's mother would be willing to sign legal papers taking responsibility for you. What other ideas do you have?

C: Well, I guess that's all I have for now.

P: If you have other ideas of how to make this work, I'll be glad to hear them. I really don't want us to have to split up. I just don't know what else to do.

In this situation, the parent is not saying that she *will not* put up with the way the child has been acting. She is saying that she *cannot* put up with it anymore. It is not a power position. It is a weak position. She is not scolding, blaming, or inviting a fight. The two of them may be able to work out this particular problem, and it may be the first time they have been able to cooperate. Their splitting up, then, can actually be the impetus and beginning of a new, more civil and rewarding relationship.

When children in this situation are asked where they may want to live, they usually come up with unrealistic, poor choices. It is a strong invitation for the parent to get into an argument. The mother in the above example expressed her concerns about the choices but did not immediately negate them. Often, reality helps make decisions. The father in the above example may not be able to take the child. The friend's parent may not be willing to take the child when faced with the responsibilities that come with him. There may be other legal ramifications that, when discovered, make any other placement very difficult.

Throughout this "exploring alternatives process," the parent is staying in a *helpful, concerned* role. It is not the parent who is inhibiting the child's plans. It is reality. Reality is hard to fight. Sometimes, because the parent has stayed out of the fight and let reality do the talking, the child realizes that he has no other real options. He is then in the position of having to decide to survive at home. He is forced to cooperate by real circumstances. Now he is making the *decision* to cooperate, though, instead of being *forced into* it by his parent. This would be an example of something working when nothing else has, and it is the usual result of "nothing working."

These situations can, however, end with the child leaving or being sent away with many bad feelings on both sides. On the other hand, if the child does find a place to stay and moves out of the house, and if the parent continues in her *helpful, concerned* role, the relationship would already be changing. Even though it seems like an ending or a bad solution to a bad problem, it can be the beginning of a new, better relationship.

With Strategic Interaction the feelings can be positive, even on departure. It may be the first time in years the parent and child have had such feelings. With this positive experience and the physical distance, a new relationship can begin.

Things to Think About When Things Seem Hopeless

❏ Get out of the *power position*, but be firm.

❏ Let *reality* be the villain. Reality is the only real power.

❏ The important thing here is to change the interaction. It may not be possible to change the child or the situation at this time.

❏ Think of it as an opportunity to start over on a more positive, effective relationship.

❏ Parenting is not something you **do to** a child; it's a relationship you have **with** a child.

What they perceive as an impossible and painful situation calling for professional intervention is simply the complexity of human life [and growing up in it].

—Thomas Moore,
Care of the Soul (1992)

There is trust that nature heals, and that much can be accomplished by not-doing.

—Thomas Moore,
Care of the Soul (1992)

Chapter 19

When "Nothing" Works, This Works

When nothing works, Strategic Interaction works! Even in the example where the child wanted to leave home, with Strategic Interaction a new relationship could emerge. This does not mean that a perfect solution occurred immediately.

Think about the following points:

❏ Relationships take time to build (or rebuild).

❏ Change often occurs slowly.

❏ Your *child* is a developing *person.* Parents have the tendency to think of their children as "things" instead of human beings.

❏ In 20 years, it will make no difference whatsoever how your child wore his hair or that he said something rude or even that he was suspended from school.

❏ There is no research that shows that rebellious youth always turn out to be unsuccessful, unhappy adults.

❏ Much of the trouble children get into is considered "status offenses." If they did the same thing at age 21 that they are in trouble for at age 15, little notice would be given.

❏ The cocky self-confidence, the refusal to be controlled, and the rebelliousness against an authority they believe to be unfair can be positive qualities when children get older. These qualities may make them strong businesspeople, politicians interested in change, or just generally creative, assertive people.

❏ **Most children grow up to be fairly good people. Maturity cures many difficult children.**

Strategic Interaction may not seem like a powerful tool, but it is the most powerful approach you can use. Look back over the Parent's Creed. Concentrate on it. Practice it. Look at the immediate consequences of Strategic Interaction. When you practice Strategic Interaction and you see your child stop because you have thrown him a curve, you will feel the power of being in control of the interaction. You will then be encouraged to try more. You can't be perfect all the time, so don't expect it or put yourself down when you make a mistake.

Learn to relax! Learn to enjoy yourself and your child. In 99 percent of the situations I have encountered, the parents have done a much better job teaching their children than they think they have. The parents now have only to interact in such a way that the child will act on those lessons. No matter what happens, when the child matures and gets a family of his own, the lessons will be evident then.

Things to Think About When Looking at Your Relationships

❑ Strategic Interaction is a powerful tool, even though it doesn't use power.

❑ Be in control of *interactions*, not your child.

❑ Your child probably already has all your lessons stored in his brain. Now you have to interact in such a way that allows the lessons to come out and allows him to use them.

Here's to Strategic Interactions and new relationships!

Recommended Reading

Good ideas are to be found in many parenting books. All of the major ones, and some of the minor ones, stress having control without necessarily having power. Descriptions of parent-child dynamics may vary. Recommended strategies for change may differ. But all seem to converge at pretty much the same point: **effective parenting takes the place of overpowering the child.**

The books included below have been chosen for their clarity, easiness to read, treatment of important points, and/or how they fit or complement the Strategic Interaction approach. The list is not meant to be exhaustive or even to represent the best in the field. While these are good, you may find others to be useful as well. I suggest that you read everything you can. You cannot read or hear about effective parenting strategies too many times. Parenting is so difficult that one must take "refresher courses" as often as possible.

Cline, F. and J. Fay. (1992). *Parenting Teens with Love and Logic.* Colorado Springs, CO: Piñon Press.

These authors offer many good insights into parent-teen relationships and give examples to illustrate their points. Their emphasis is on changing how parents deal with problems, not on controlling the children.

Dinkmeyer, D. and G. McKay. (1989). *The Parent's Handbook: Systematic Training for Effective Parenting (STEP).* Circle Pines, MN: American Guidance Service, Inc.

This book, and the video training that accompanies it, has been used in many parent education groups. I especially like the authors' treatment of natural and logical consequences.

Dreikers, R. (1964). *Children: The Challenge.* New York, NY: Plume Books.

This is one of the original classics. The ideas of logical and natural consequences, respect for the child, and firmness without domination have been repeated in many books since appearing in this one. Some of the other books reviewed treat these concepts with more conciseness and clarity, though.

Faber, E. and E. Mazlisch. (1980). *How to Talk So Kids Will Listen and Listen So Kids Will Talk.* New York, NY: Avon Books.

This is an enjoyable book to read, and the message is good to hear and learn. The authors are very good at helping the reader interact with his children in a way similar to the Strategic Interaction approach.

Ginott, H. (1969). *Between Parent and Teenager.* New York, NY: Avon Books.

Faber and Mazlisch used Dr. Ginott's ideas as the foundation for their book. The ideas are good and there are many easy-to-follow examples. You may find that Faber and Mazlisch present the ideas in a more interesting way.

Gordon, T. (1970). *Parent Effectiveness Training.* New York, NY: Penguin Books.

This is one of the "classics." I especially like the sections on active listening and the relationship between parental authority and teenage rebellion. It also discusses what can and cannot be effected by parents and parenting.

Leftin, H. (1990). *The Family Contract: A Blueprint for Successful Parenting.* Summit, NJ: PIA Press.

This book was written by a psychiatrist in the Houston area and may be hard to find, but it deals very well with a way to set up discipline and rules that helps parents stay out of battles over those rules.

Popkin, M. (1993). *Active Parenting Today: The Basics.* Marietta, GA: Active Parenting Publishing.

Popkin, M. (1990). *Active Parenting of Teens: A Video-Based Program for Parents of Teens.* Marietta, GA: Active Parenting Publishing.

A structured video training program was developed to accompany the book. The video is very entertaining and the points are well illustrated. I especially like the author's treatment of the important concept of "problem ownership."

Rosemond, J. (1990). *Ending the Homework Hassle.* Kansas City, MO: Andrews and McMeel.

Rosemond, J. (1997). *Rosemond's 8-Point Plan for Raising Happy, Healthy Children.* Kansas City, MO: Andrews and McMeel.

I consider John Rosemond controversial because he takes a no-nonsense approach to parenting. He seems to emphasize the Business side and does not mention the Personal side enough. Although the way he says some things seems harsh, the more I read of his work, the more I believe that he has important things to say about dealing with teens.

The following books are about treating difficult behavior problems in agencies such as schools and youth centers. The philosophy they promote in dealing with kids in order to make a difference is much like what I promote in this book. This way of thinking about children is important for parents to adopt in their dealings with their children.

Bendtro, L., M. Brokenleg & S. Van Brocken. (1990). *Reclaiming Youth at Risk: Our Hope for the Future.* Bloomington, IN: National Educational Service.

Curwin, R. and A. Mendler. (1988). *Discipline with Dignity.* Reston, VA: Association for Supervision and Curriculum Development.

Mendler, A. (1992). *What Do I Do When: How to Achieve Discipline with Dignity in the Classroom.* Bloomington, IN: National Educational Service.

Ordering Information

Would you like to order extra copies for a friend or pass a book along to family members?

Additional copies of *Raising Children You Can Live With* are available from the publisher. Orders can be placed by phone, by mail, or by FAX.

❏ *To order by mail:* Complete this order form and mail it (along with check or credit card information) to Bayou Publishing, 2524 Nottingham, Houston, TX 77005-1412.

❏ *To order by phone:* Call (800) 340-2034.

❏ *To order by FAX:* Fill out this order form (including credit card information) and fax to (713) 526-4342.

Name:_____

Address: _____

_____

City: _____   ST:_____   Zip:_____

Ph: _____

FAX: _____

❏ VISA   ❏ MasterCard   ❏ American Express

Charge Card #: _____

Expiration Date:_____

Signature: _____

Please send me _____ copies at $14.95 each $ _____

plus $2.50 postage and handling *(per order)* $2.50

                                     Total $_____

Bayou Publishing
2524 Nottingham, Suite 150
Houston, TX 77005-1412
Ph: (713) 526-4558/ FAX: (713) 526-4342
Orders: (800) 340-2034
http://www.bayoupublishing.com

About the Author

Photo: Rick Goncher

Jamie Raser, LMSW-ACP, has been working with children and their families since 1976. His clinical skills have been sought by children's protection agencies, juvenile probation units, schools, and family doctors. He is a licensed master of social work–advanced clinical practitioner and a licensed marriage and family therapist. Jamie has been a clinical faculty member of the Houston Galveston Institute since 1986 and currently serves on the Psychological and Counseling Services staff of Deer Park Independent School District, Deer Park, Texas. He also serves on the editorial advisory board for the *Journal of Systemic Therapies.*

Jamie maintains a clinical practice in Houston and conducts workshops internationally on parenting and adolescent issues. He believes that it is possible to raise children you can live with and to have fun doing it.